The National Curriculum in England

Key Stages 1 and 2 framework document

Contents

Letter from Scholastic   3

1. Introduction   4

2. The school curriculum in England   4

3. The National Curriculum in England   5

4. Inclusion   7

5. Numeracy and mathematics   8

6. Language and literacy   8

7. The Programmes of Study and Attainment targets for the National Curriculum subjects

- English

- Mathematics

- Science

- Art and design

- Computing

- Design and technology

- Geography

- History

- Languages

- Music

- Physical Education

SCHOLASTIC

Book End, Range Road, Witney, Oxfordshire, OX29 OYD

www.scholastic.co.uk

© 2013, Scholastic Ltd

1 2 3 4 5 6 7 8 9   0 1 2 3 4 5 6 7 8 9

British Library Cataloguing-in-Publication Data
A catalogue record for this book is available from the
British Library.

ISBN 978-1407-12862-7
Printed by Ashford Colour Press Ltd, Gosport, Hants

Every effort has been made to trace copyright holders
for the works reproduced in this book, and the
publishers apologise for any inadvertent omissions.

Extracts from The National Curriculum in England for
Key Stages 1-2 © Crown Copyright. Reproduced under
the terms of the Open Government Licence (OGL)
www.nationalarchives.gov.uk/doc/open-government-
licence/open-government-licence.htm

▟ SCHOLASTIC

Euston House, 24 Eversholt Street, London NW1 1DB, UK

Website: www.scholastic.co.uk

Dear Teacher

Earlier this year, the Department for Education released the new *National Curriculum for England* on their website. At Scholastic, we are constantly talking to teachers and know that a printed version of the Curriculum is a useful tool that you can annotate and carry with you when you plan your lessons. We decided that as a 'thank you' to teachers for your years of supporting our education resources, book fairs and book clubs in schools, we would send a free copy of the Curriculum to your school.

We know that there is no job more important than teaching and we work hard to publish the best resources to support you and help you deliver a rich and creative primary curriculum for the children you teach.

To help you deliver the new National Curriculum for England, we are publishing new 100 Lesson Plans and Planning Guide resources for English, Maths, Science, History, Geography and Computing. These resources are a creative, exciting way to teach the new Curriculum whilst giving you all the professional development support you need. They are part of the bestselling series of teacher resources that have supported teachers since the introduction of the Literacy Hour in 1998 with over 1 million copies sold.

I hope that you find this publication useful, and wish you the very best for the year ahead.

Catherine Bell.

Catherine Bell
Co-Group Managing Director, Scholastic

Registered Office: Scholastic Ltd., Westfield Road, Southam, Warwickshire CV47 0RA. Registered in England No. 701339 Vat No. GB241359376

If you would like more copies of this publication, would like to discuss any of our new resources, or would like to book one of our Educational Sales Consultants to visit you in school, please call us on 0845 603 9091

1. Introduction

1.1 This document sets out the framework for the National Curriculum at Key Stages 1 and 2, and includes:

- contextual information about both the overall school curriculum and the statutory National Curriculum, including the statutory basis of the latter
- aims for the statutory National Curriculum
- statements on inclusion, and on the development of pupils' competence in numeracy and mathematics, language and literacy across the school curriculum
- Programmes of Study for all the National Curriculum subjects that are taught at Key Stages 1 and 2.

2. The school curriculum in England

2.1 Every state-funded school must offer a curriculum which is balanced and broadly based[1] and which:

- promotes the spiritual, moral, cultural, mental and physical development of pupils at the school and of society, and
- prepares pupils at the school for the opportunities, responsibilities and experiences of later life.

2.2 The school curriculum comprises all learning and other experiences that each school plans for its pupils. The National Curriculum forms one part of the school curriculum.

2.3 All state schools are also required to make provision for a daily act of collective worship and must teach religious education to pupils at every key stage and sex and relationship education to pupils in secondary education.

2.4 Maintained schools in England are legally required to follow the statutory National Curriculum which sets out in Programmes of Study, on the basis of key stages, subject content for those subjects that should be taught to all pupils. All schools must publish their school curriculum by subject and academic year online.[2]

2.5 All schools should make provision for personal, social, health and economic education (PSHE), drawing on good practice. Schools are also free to include other subjects or topics of their choice in planning and designing their own programme of education.

---

[1] See Section 78 of the 2002 Education Act: http://www.legislation.gov.uk/ukpga/2002/32/section/78 which applies to all maintained schools. Academies are also required to offer a broad and balanced curriculum in accordance with Section 1 of the 2010 Academies Act; http://www.legislation.gov.uk/ukpga/2010/32/section/1

[2] From September 2012, all schools are required to publish information in relation to each academic year, relating to the content of the school's curriculum for each subject and details about how additional information relating to the curriculum may be obtained: http://www.legislation.gov.uk/uksi/2012/1124/made.

3. The National Curriculum in England

Aims

3.1 The National Curriculum provides pupils with an introduction to the essential knowledge that they need to be educated citizens. It introduces pupils to the best that has been thought and said; and helps engender an appreciation of human creativity and achievement.

3.2 The National Curriculum is just one element in the education of every child. There is time and space in the school day and in each week, term and year to range beyond the National Curriculum specifications. The National Curriculum provides an outline of core knowledge around which teachers can develop exciting and stimulating lessons to promote the development of pupils' knowledge, understanding and skills as part of the wider school curriculum.

Structure

3.3 Pupils of compulsory school age in community and foundation schools, including community special schools and foundation special schools, and in voluntary aided and voluntary controlled schools, must follow the National Curriculum. It is organised on the basis of four key stages[3] and twelve subjects, classified in legal terms as 'core' and 'other foundation' subjects.

3.4 The Secretary of State for Education is required to publish Programmes of Study for each National Curriculum subject, setting out the 'matters, skills and processes' to be taught at each key stage. Schools are free to choose how they organise their school day, as long as the content of National Curriculum Programmes of Study is taught to all pupils.

---

[3] The Key Stage 2 Programmes of Study for English, mathematics and science are presented in this document as 'lower' (Years 3 and 4) and 'upper' (Years 5 and 6). This distinction is made as guidance for teachers and is not reflected in legislation. The legal requirement is to cover the content of the Programmes of Study for Years 3 to 6 by the end of Key Stage 2.

3.5 The proposed structure of the new National Curriculum, in terms of which subjects are compulsory at each key stage, is set out in the table below:

Figure 1 – Structure of the National Curriculum

	Key Stage 1	Key Stage 2	Key Stage 3	Key Stage 4
Age	5 – 7	7 – 11	11 – 14	14 – 16
Year groups	1 – 2	3 – 6	7 – 9	10 – 11
Core subjects				
English	✓	✓	✓	✓
Mathematics	✓	✓	✓	✓
Science	✓	✓	✓	✓
Foundation subjects				
Art and design	✓	✓	✓	
Citizenship			✓	✓
Computing	✓	✓	✓	✓
Design and technology	✓	✓	✓	
Languages[4]		✓	✓	
Geography	✓	✓	✓	
History	✓	✓	✓	
Music	✓	✓	✓	
Physical education	✓	✓	✓	✓

3.6 All schools are also required to teach religious education at all key stages.

Secondary schools must provide sex and relationship education.

Figure 2 – Statutory teaching of religious education and sex and relationship education

	Key stage 1	Key stage 2	Key stage 3	Key stage 4
Age		7 – 11	11 – 14	14 – 16
Year groups	1 – 2	3 – 6	7 – 9	10 – 11
Religious education	✓	✓	✓	✓
Sex and relationship education			✓	✓

---

[4] At Key Stage 2 the subject title is 'foreign language'; at key stage 3 it is 'modern foreign language'.

■SCHOLASTIC

4. Inclusion

Setting suitable challenges

4.1   Teachers should set high expectations for every pupil. They should plan stretching work for children whose attainment is significantly above the expected standard. They have an even greater obligation to plan lessons for pupils who have low levels of prior attainment or come from disadvantaged backgrounds. Teachers should use appropriate assessment to set targets which are deliberately ambitious.

Responding to pupils' needs and overcoming potential barriers for individuals and groups of pupils

4.2   Teachers should take account of their duties under equal opportunities legislation that covers race, disability, sex, religion or belief, sexual orientation, pregnancy and maternity, and gender assessment.

4.3   A wide range of pupils have special educational needs, many of whom also have disabilities. Lessons should be planned to ensure that there are no barriers to every child achieving. In many cases, such planning will mean that these pupils will be able to study the full National Curriculum. The SEN Code of Practice will include advice on approaches to identification of need which can support this. A minority of pupils will need access to specialist equipment and different approaches. The SEN Code of Practice will outline what needs to be done for them.

4.4   With the right teaching that recognises their individual needs, many disabled pupils have little need for additional resources beyond the aids which they use as part of their daily life. Teachers must plan lessons so that these pupils can study every National Curriculum subject. Potential areas of difficulty should be identified and addressed at the outset of work.

4.5   Teachers must also take account of the needs of pupils whose first language is not English. Monitoring of progress should take account of the child's age, length of time in this country, previous educational experience and ability in other languages.

4.6   The ability of pupils for whom English is an additional language to take part in the National Curriculum may be in advance of their communication skills in English. Teachers should plan teaching opportunities to help pupils develop their English and should aim to provide the support pupils need to take part in all subjects.

---

[5] Age is a protected characteristic under the Equality Act 2010 but it is not applicable to schools in relation to education or (as far as relating to those under the age of 18) the provision of services; it is a relevant protected characteristic in relation to the provision of services or employment (so when thinking about staff). Marriage and civil partnership are also a protected characteristic but only in relation to employment.

5. Numeracy and mathematics

5.1   Teachers should use every relevant subject to develop pupils' mathematical fluency. Confidence in numeracy and other mathematical skills is a precondition of success across the National Curriculum

5.2   Teachers should develop pupils' numeracy and mathematical reasoning in all subjects so that they understand and appreciate the importance of mathematics. Pupils should be taught to apply arithmetic fluently to problems, understand and use measures, make estimates and sense check their work. Pupils should apply their geometric and algebraic understanding, and relate their understanding of probability to the notions of risk and uncertainty. They should also understand the cycle of collecting, presenting and analysing data. They should be taught to apply their mathematics to both routine and non-routine problems, including breaking down more complex problems into a series of simpler steps.

6. Language and literacy

6.1   Teachers should develop pupils' spoken language, reading, writing and vocabulary as integral aspects of the teaching of every subject. English is both a subject in its own right and the medium for teaching; for pupils, understanding the language provides access to the whole curriculum. Fluency in the English language is an essential foundation for success in all subjects.

Spoken language

6.2   Pupils should be taught to speak clearly and convey ideas confidently using Standard English. They should learn to justify ideas with reasons; ask questions to check understanding; develop vocabulary and build knowledge; negotiate; evaluate and build on the ideas of others; and select the appropriate register for effective communication. They should be taught to give well-structured descriptions and explanations and develop their understanding through speculating, hypothesising and exploring ideas. This will enable them to clarify their thinking as well as organise their ideas for writing.

Reading and writing

6.3   Teachers should develop pupils' reading and writing in all subjects to support their acquisition of knowledge. Pupils should be taught to read fluently, understand extended prose (both fiction and non-fiction) and be encouraged to read for pleasure. Schools should do everything to promote wider reading. They should provide library facilities and set ambitious expectations for reading at home. Pupils should develop the stamina and skills to write at length, with accurate spelling and punctuation. They should be taught the correct use of grammar. They should build on what they have been taught to expand the range of their writing and the variety of the grammar they use. The writing they do should include narratives, explanations, descriptions, comparisons, summaries and evaluations: such writing supports them in rehearsing, understanding and consolidating what they have heard or read.

Vocabulary development

6.4 Pupils' acquisition and command of vocabulary are key to their learning and progress across the whole curriculum. Teachers should therefore develop vocabulary actively, building systematically on pupils' current knowledge. They should increase pupils' store of words in general; simultaneously, they should also make links between known and new vocabulary and discuss the shades of meaning in similar words. In this way, pupils expand the vocabulary choices that are available to them when they write. In addition, it is vital for pupils' comprehension that they understand the meanings of words they meet in their reading across all subjects, and older pupils should be taught the meaning of instruction verbs that they may meet in examination questions. It is particularly important to induct pupils into the language which defines each subject in its own right, such as accurate mathematical and scientific language.

7. Programmes of Study and Attainment targets

7.1 The following pages set out the proposed statutory Programmes of Study for all subjects at Key Stages 1 - 2. Where content is shown in grey text, it is 'non-statutory'.

WHAT'S NEW
IN THE 2014 CURRICULUM?

- Year–by-year programmes for Key Stage 1
- The principles of systematic phonics in the early teaching of reading
- New Spelling Appendix (see pages 41-54)
- New Vocabulary, Grammar and Punctuation Appendix (see pages 56 - 73)
- Strong focus on children reading widely and often
- Spoken language requirements apply to all year groups.

Scholastic resources that support the 2014 English Curriculum

100 English Lessons

100 English Lessons for the 2014 Curriculum brings you a whole year of inspirational ready-made lessons fully matched to the new curriculum.

- Master the new curriculum: every lesson is carefully matched to the new objectives
- A whole year planned and ready to teach
- Time-saving pick-up-and-use format
- A trusted series: over a million copies sold

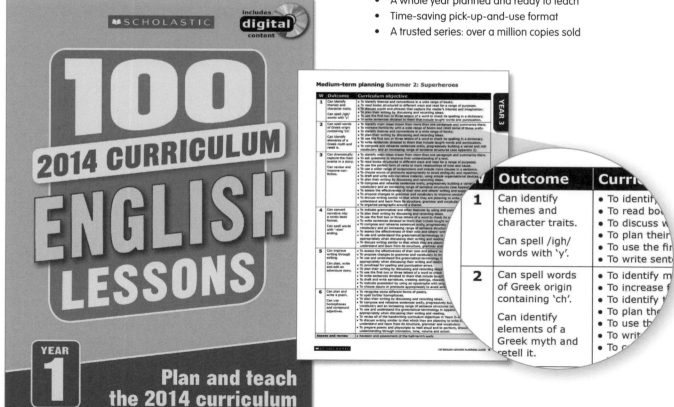

SCHOLASTIC

Connectors

Connectors is a ground-breaking reading series which supports disadvantaged learners and narrows the attainment gap through evidence-based peer-to-peer learning.

- Supports the reciprocal reading approach
- Children work in small independent groups, taking turns to lead as they read together, following prompts to make predictions and debate issues raised in the text
- Fosters a love of reading by rapidly developing reading comprehension and fuelling curiosity and imagination

Read & Respond

Read & Respond is an ideal alternative to reading schemes or extract-based reading, letting children discover the joys of real classic children's novels and books.

- Richly immersive approach creates efficient and responsive readers
- Helps to foster a reading habit that lasts a lifetime

English

Purpose of study

English has a pre-eminent place in education and in society. A high-quality education in English will teach pupils to write and speak fluently so that they can communicate their ideas and emotions to others and through their reading and listening, others can communicate with them. Through reading in particular, pupils have a chance to develop culturally, emotionally, intellectually, socially and spiritually. Literature, especially, plays a key role in such development. Reading also enables pupils both to acquire knowledge and to build on what they already know. All the skills of language are essential to participating fully as a member of society; pupils, therefore, who do not learn to speak, read and write fluently and confidently are effectively disenfranchised.

Aims

The overarching aim for English in the National Curriculum is to promote high standards of literacy by equipping pupils with a strong command of the spoken and written word, and to develop their love of literature through widespread reading for enjoyment. The National Curriculum for English aims to ensure that all pupils:

- read easily, fluently and with good understanding
- develop the habit of reading widely and often, for both pleasure and information
- acquire a wide vocabulary, an understanding of grammar and knowledge of linguistic conventions for reading, writing and spoken language
- appreciate our rich and varied literary heritage
- write clearly, accurately and coherently, adapting their language and style in and for a range of contexts, purposes and audiences
- use discussion in order to learn; they should be able to elaborate and explain clearly their understanding and ideas
- are competent in the arts of speaking and listening, making formal presentations, demonstrating to others and participating in debate.

Spoken language

The National Curriculum for English reflects the importance of spoken language in pupils' development across the whole curriculum – cognitively, socially and linguistically. Spoken language underpins the development of reading and writing. The quality and variety of language that pupils hear and speak are vital for developing their vocabulary and grammar and their understanding for reading and writing. Teachers should therefore ensure the continual development of pupils' confidence and competence in spoken language and listening skills.

Pupils should develop a capacity to explain their understanding of books and other reading, and to prepare their ideas before they write. They must be assisted in making their thinking clear to themselves as well as to others and teachers should ensure that pupils build secure foundations by using discussion to probe and remedy their misconceptions. Pupils should also be taught to understand and use the conventions for discussion and debate.

All pupils should be enabled to participate in and gain knowledge, skills and understanding associated with the artistic practice of drama. Pupils should be able to adopt, create and sustain a range of roles, responding appropriately to others in role. They should have opportunities to improvise, devise and script drama for one another and a range of audiences, as well as to rehearse, refine, share and respond thoughtfully to drama and theatre performances.

Statutory requirements which underpin all aspects of speaking and listening across the six years of primary education form part of the National Curriculum. These are reflected and contextualised within the reading and writing domains which follow.

Reading

The Programmes of Study for reading at Key Stages 1 and 2 consist of two dimensions:

- word reading
- comprehension (both listening and reading).

It is essential that teaching focuses on developing pupils' competence in both dimensions; different kinds of teaching are needed for each.

Skilled word reading involves both the speedy working out of the pronunciation of unfamiliar printed words (decoding) and the speedy recognition of familiar printed words. Underpinning both is the understanding that the letters on the page represent the sounds in spoken words. This is why phonics should be emphasised in the early teaching of reading to beginners (ie unskilled readers) when they start school.

Good comprehension draws from linguistic knowledge (in particular of vocabulary and grammar) and on knowledge of the world. Comprehension skills develop through pupils' experience of high-quality discussion with the teacher, as well as from reading and discussing a range of stories, poems and non-fiction. All pupils must be encouraged to read widely across both fiction and non-fiction to develop their knowledge of themselves and the world in which they live, to establish an appreciation and love of reading, and to gain knowledge across the curriculum. Reading widely and often increases pupils' vocabulary because they encounter words they would rarely hear or use in everyday speech. Reading also feeds pupils' imagination and opens up a treasure-house of wonder and joy for curious young minds.

It is essential that, by the end of their primary education, all pupils are able to read fluently, and with confidence, in any subject in their forthcoming secondary education.

Writing

The Programmes of Study for writing at Key Stages 1 and 2 are constructed similarly to those for reading:

- transcription (spelling and handwriting)
- composition (articulating ideas and structuring them in speech and writing).

It is essential that teaching develops pupils' competence in these two dimensions. In addition, pupils should be taught how to plan, revise and evaluate their writing. These aspects of writing have been incorporated into the Programmes of Study for composition.

Writing down ideas fluently depends on effective transcription: that is, on spelling quickly and accurately through knowing the relationship between sounds and letters (phonics) and understanding the morphology (word structure) and orthography (spelling structure) of words. Effective composition involves articulating and communicating ideas, and then organising them coherently for a reader. This requires clarity, awareness of the audience, purpose and context, and an increasingly wide knowledge of vocabulary and grammar. Writing also depends on fluent, legible and, eventually, speedy handwriting.

Spelling, vocabulary, grammar, punctuation and glossary

The two statutory appendices – on spelling and on vocabulary, grammar and punctuation – give an overview of the specific features that should be included in teaching the Programme of Study.

Opportunities for teachers to enhance pupils' vocabulary arise naturally from their reading and writing. As vocabulary increases, teachers should show pupils how to understand the relationships between words, how to understand nuances in meaning, and how to develop their understanding of, and ability to use, figurative language. They should also teach pupils how to work out and clarify the meanings of unknown words and words with more than one meaning. References to developing pupils' vocabulary are also included within the appendices.

Pupils should be taught to control their speaking and writing consciously and to use Standard English. They should be taught to use the elements of spelling, grammar, punctuation and 'language about language' listed. This is not intended to constrain or restrict teachers' creativity, but simply to provide the structure on which they can construct exciting lessons. A non-statutory glossary is provided for teachers. Throughout the Programme of Study, teachers should teach pupils the vocabulary they need to discuss their reading, writing and spoken language. It is important that pupils learn the correct grammatical terms in English and that these terms are integrated within teaching.

School curriculum

The Programme of Study for English are set out year-by-year for Key Stage 1 and two-yearly for Key Stage 2. The single year blocks at Key Stage 1 reflect the rapid pace of development in word reading during these two years. Schools are, however, only required to teach the relevant Programme of Study by the end of the Key Stage. Within each key stage, schools therefore have the flexibility to introduce content earlier or later than set out in the Programme of Study. In addition, schools can introduce content during an earlier key stage if appropriate.

All schools are also required to set out their school curriculum for English on a year-by-year basis and make this information available online.

Attainment targets

By the end of each key stage, pupils are expected to know, apply and understand the matters, skills and processes specified in the relevant Programme of Study.

Schools are not required by law to teach the example content in grey or the content indicated as being 'non-statutory'.

English Programme of Study: Spoken Language – Years 1–6

Programme of Study (statutory requirements)	Notes and guidance (non-statutory)
SPOKEN LANGUAGE Pupils should be taught to: • listen and respond appropriately to adults and their peers • ask relevant questions to extend their understanding and knowledge • use relevant strategies to build their vocabulary • articulate and justify answers, arguments and opinions • give well-structured descriptions, explanations and narratives for different purposes, including for expressing feelings • maintain attention and participate actively in collaborative conversations, staying on topic and initiating and responding to comments • use spoken language to develop understanding through speculating, hypothesising, imagining and exploring ideas • speak audibly and fluently with an increasing command of Standard English • participate in discussions, presentations, performances, role play, improvisations and debates • gain, maintain and monitor the interest of the listener(s) • consider and evaluate different viewpoints, attending to and building on the contributions of others • select and use appropriate registers for effective communication.	**SPOKEN LANGUAGE** These statements apply to all years. The content should be taught at a level appropriate to the age of the pupils. Pupils should build on the oral language skills that have been taught in preceding years. Pupils should be taught to develop their competence in spoken language and listening to enhance the effectiveness with which they are able to communicate across a range of contexts and to a range of audiences. They should therefore have opportunities to work in groups of different sizes – in pairs, small, large groups and as a whole class. Pupils should understand how to take turns and when and how to participate constructively in conversations and debates. Attention should also be paid to increasing pupils' vocabulary, ranging from describing their immediate world and feelings to developing a broader, deeper and richer vocabulary to discuss abstract concepts and a wider range of topics, and to their knowledge about language as a whole. Pupils should receive constructive feedback on their spoken language and listening not only to improve their knowledge and skills but also to establish secure foundations for effective spoken language in their studies at primary school, helping them to achieve in secondary education and beyond.

Key Stage 1

Year 1

During Year 1, teachers should build on work from the Early Years Foundation Stage, making sure that pupils can sound and blend unfamiliar printed words quickly and accurately using the phonic knowledge and skills that they have already learned. Teachers should also ensure that pupils continue to learn new grapheme-phoneme correspondences (GPCs) and revise and consolidate those learned earlier. The understanding that the letter(s) on the page represent the sounds in spoken words should underpin pupils' reading and spelling of all words. This includes common words containing unusual GPCs. The term 'common exception words' is used throughout the Programmes of Study for such words.

Alongside this knowledge of GPCs, pupils need to develop the skill of blending the sounds into words for reading and establish the habit of applying this skill whenever they encounter new words. This will be supported by practising their reading with books consistent with their developing phonic knowledge and skill and their knowledge of common exception words. At the same time they will need to hear, share and discuss a wide range of high-quality books to develop a love of reading and broaden their vocabulary.

Pupils should be helped to read words without overt sounding and blending after a few encounters. Those who are slow to develop this skill should have extra practice.

Pupils' writing during Year 1 will generally develop at a slower pace than their reading. This is because they need to encode the sounds they hear in words (spelling skills), develop the physical skill needed for handwriting, and learn how to organise their ideas in writing.

Pupils entering Year 1 who have not yet met the early learning goals for literacy should continue to follow their school's curriculum or the Early Years Foundation Stage to develop their word reading, spelling and language skills. However, these pupils should follow the Year 1 Programme of Study in terms of the books they listen to and discuss, so that they develop their vocabulary and understanding of grammar, as well as their knowledge more generally across the curriculum. If they are still struggling to decode and spell, they need to be taught to do this urgently through a rigorous and systematic phonics programme so that they catch up rapidly.

Teachers should ensure that their teaching develops pupils' oral vocabulary as well as their ability to understand and use a variety of grammatical structures, giving particular support to pupils whose oral language skills are insufficiently developed.

Year 1 Programme of Study (statutory requirements)

READING

Word reading

Pupils should be taught to:

- apply phonic knowledge and skills as the route to decode words
- respond speedily with the correct sound to graphemes (letters or groups of letters) for all 40+ phonemes, including, where applicable, alternative sounds for graphemes
- read accurately by blending sounds in unfamiliar words containing GPCs that have been taught
- read common exception words, noting unusual correspondences between spelling and sound and where these occur in the word
- read words containing taught GPCs and -s, -es, -ing, -ed, -er and -est endings
- read other words of more than one syllable that contain taught GPCs
- read words with contractions, (for example *I'm, I'll, we'll*), and understand that the apostrophe represents the omitted letter(s)
- read aloud accurately books that are consistent with their developing phonic knowledge and that do not require them to use other strategies to work out words
- re-read these books to build up their fluency and confidence in word reading.

Notes and guidance (non-statutory)

READING

Word reading

Pupils should revise and consolidate the GPCs and the common exception words taught in Reception. As soon as they can read words comprising the Year 1 GPCs accurately and speedily, they should move on to the Year 2 Programme of Study for word reading.

The number, order and choice of exception words taught will vary according to the phonics programme being used. Ensuring that pupils are aware of the GPCs they contain, however unusual these are, supports spelling later.

Young readers encounter words that they have not seen before much more frequently than experienced readers do, and they may not know the meaning of some of these. Practice at reading such words by sounding and blending can provide opportunities not only for pupils to develop confidence in their decoding skills, but also for teachers to explain the meaning and thus develop pupils' vocabulary.

Pupils should be taught how to read words with suffixes by being helped to build on the root words that they can read already. Pupils' reading and re-reading of books that are closely matched to their developing phonic knowledge and knowledge of common exception words supports their fluency, as well as increasing their confidence in their reading skills. Fluent word reading greatly assists comprehension, especially when pupils come to read longer books.

Year 1 Programme of Study (statutory requirements)	Notes and guidance (non-statutory)

READING
 	
Comprehension
 	
Pupils should be taught to:
 	
• develop pleasure in reading, motivation to read, vocabulary and understanding by:
 	
   • listening to and discussing a wide range of poems, stories and non-fiction at a level beyond that at which they can read independently
 	
   • being encouraged to link what they read or hear read to their own experiences
 	
   • becoming very familiar with key stories, fairy stories and traditional tales, retelling them and considering their particular characteristics
 	
   • recognising and joining in with predictable phrases
 	
   • learning to appreciate rhymes and poems, and to recite some by heart
 	
   • discussing word meanings, linking new meanings to those already known
 	
• understand both the books they can already read accurately and fluently and those they listen to by:
 	
   • drawing on what they already know or on background information and vocabulary provided by the teacher
 	
   • checking that the text makes sense to them as they read and correcting inaccurate reading
 	
   • discussing the significance of the title and events
 	
   • making inferences on the basis of what is being said and done
 	
   • predicting what might happen on the basis of what has been read so far
 	
• participate in discussion about what is read to them, taking turns and listening to what others say
 	
• explain clearly their understanding of what is read to them.
	READING
	
	Comprehension
	
	Pupils should have extensive experience of listening to, sharing and discussing a wide range of high-quality books with the teacher, other adults and each other to engender a love of reading at the same time as they are reading independently.
	
	Pupils' vocabulary should be developed when they listen to books read aloud and when they discuss what they have heard. Such vocabulary can also feed into their writing. Knowing the meaning of more words increases pupils' chances of understanding when they read by themselves. The meaning of some new words should be introduced to pupils before they start to read on their own, so that these unknown words do not hold up their comprehension.
	
	However, once pupils have already decoded words successfully, the meaning of those that are new to them can be discussed with them, so contributing to developing their early skills of inference. By listening frequently to stories, poems and non-fiction that they cannot yet read for themselves, pupils begin to understand how written language can be structured in order, for example, how to build surprise in narratives or to present facts in non-fiction. Listening to and discussing information books and other non-fiction establishes the foundations for their learning in other subjects. Pupils should be shown some of the processes for finding out information.
	
	Through listening, pupils also start to learn how language sounds and increase their vocabulary and awareness of grammatical structures.
	
	In due course, they will be able to draw on such grammar in their own writing.
	
	Rules for effective discussions should be agreed with and demonstrated for children. They should help to develop and evaluate them, with the expectation that everyone takes part. Pupils should be helped to consider the opinions of others.
	
	Roleplay can help pupils to identify with and explore characters and to try out the language they have listened to.

Year 1 Programme of Study (statutory requirements)	Notes and guidance (non-statutory)
WRITING	**WRITING**
Transcription	**Transcription**
Spelling (see English Appendix 1)	*Spelling*
Pupils should be taught to:	Reading should be taught alongside spelling, so that pupils understand that they can read back words they have spelt.
• spell:	Pupils should be shown how to segment words into individual phonemes and then how to represent the phonemes by the appropriate grapheme(s). It is important to recognise that phoneme-grapheme correspondences (which underpin spelling) are more variable than grapheme-phoneme correspondences (which underpin reading). For this reason, pupils need to do much more word-specific rehearsal for spelling than for reading.
• words containing each of the 40+ phonemes already taught	
• common exception words	
• the days of the week	
• name the letters of the alphabet:	At this stage pupils will be spelling some words in a phonically plausible way, even if sometimes incorrectly. Misspellings of words that pupils have been taught to spell should be corrected; other misspelt words should be used to teach pupils about alternative ways of representing those sounds.
• naming the letters of the alphabet in order	
• using letter names to distinguish between alternative spellings of the same sound	
• add prefixes and suffixes:	Writing simple dictated sentences that include words taught so far gives pupils opportunities to apply and practise their spelling.
• using the spelling rule for adding -s or -es as the plural marker for nouns and the third person singular marker for verbs	
• using the prefix *un-*	
• using -*ing*, -*ed*, -*er* and -*est* where no change is needed in the spelling of root words (for example, *helping, helped, helper, eating, quicker, quickest*)	
• apply simple spelling rules and guidelines, as listed in English Appendix 1	
• write from memory simple sentences dictated by the teacher that include words using the GPCs and common exception words taught so far.	

Year 1 Programme of Study (statutory requirements)	Notes and guidance (non-statutory)
Handwriting Pupils should be taught to: • sit correctly at a table, holding a pencil comfortably and correctly • begin to form lower-case letters in the correct direction, starting and finishing in the right place • form capital letters • form digits 0–9 • understand which letters belong to which handwriting 'families' (ie letters that are formed in similar ways) and to practise these.	*Handwriting* Handwriting requires frequent and discrete, direct teaching. Pupils should be able to form letters correctly and confidently. The size of the writing implement (pencil, pen) should not be too large for a young child's hand. Whatever is being used should allow the child to hold it easily and correctly so that bad habits are avoided. Left-handed pupils should receive specific teaching to meet their needs.

Composition
 	
 Pupils should be taught to:
 	
 • write sentences by:
 	
   • saying out loud what they are going to write about
 	
   • composing a sentence orally before writing it
 	
   • sequencing sentences to form short narratives
 	
   • re-reading what they have written to check that it makes sense
 	
 • discuss what they have written with the teacher or other pupils
 	
 • read aloud their writing clearly enough to be heard by their peers and the teacher.
	Composition
	
	 At the beginning of Year 1, not all pupils will have the spelling and handwriting skills they need to write down everything that they can compose out loud.
	
	 Pupils should understand, through demonstration, the skills and processes essential to writing: that is, thinking aloud as they collect ideas, drafting and re-reading to check their meaning is clear.

Year 1 Programme of Study (statutory requirements)	Notes and guidance (non-statutory)

Vocabulary, grammar and punctuation
 	
Pupils should be taught to:
 	
• develop their understanding of the concepts set out in English Appendix 2 by:
 	
  • leaving spaces between words
 	
  • joining words and joining sentences using *and*
 	
  • beginning to punctuate sentences using a capital letter and a full stop, question mark or exclamation mark
 	
  • using a capital letter for names of people, places, the days of the week, and the personal pronoun 'I'
 	
• learning the grammar for Year 1 in English Appendix 2
 	
• use the grammatical terminology in English Appendix 2 in discussing their writing.
	Vocabulary, grammar and punctuation
	
	Pupils should be taught to recognise sentence boundaries in spoken sentences and to use the vocabulary listed in English Appendix 2 ('Terminology for pupils') when their writing is discussed.
	
	Pupils should begin to use some of the distinctive features of Standard English in their writing. 'Standard English' is defined in the Glossary.

Year 2

By the beginning of Year 2, pupils should be able to read all common graphemes. They should be able to read unfamiliar words containing these graphemes, accurately and without undue hesitation, by sounding them out in books that are matched closely to each child's level of word reading knowledge. They should also be able to read many common words containing GPCs taught so far, for example, *shout*, *hand*, *stop*, or *dream*, without needing to blend the sounds out loud first. Pupils' reading of common exception words, for example, *you*, *could*, *many*, or *people*, should be secure. Pupils will increase their fluency by being able to read these words easily and automatically. Finally, pupils should be able to retell some familiar stories that have been read to and discussed with them or that they have acted out during Year 1.

During Year 2, teachers should continue to focus on establishing pupils' accurate and speedy word-reading skills. They should also make sure that pupils listen to and discuss a wide range of stories, poems, plays and information books; this should include whole books. The sooner that pupils can read well and do so frequently, the sooner they will be able to increase their vocabulary, comprehension and their knowledge across the wider curriculum.

In writing, pupils at the beginning of Year 2 should be able to compose individual sentences orally and then write them down. They should be able to spell correctly many of the words covered in Year 1 (see English Appendix 1). They should also be able to make phonically plausible attempts to spell words they have not yet learned. Finally, they should be able to form individual letters correctly, so establishing good handwriting habits from the beginning.

It is important to recognise that pupils begin to meet extra challenges in terms of spelling during Year 2. Increasingly, they should learn that there is not always an obvious connection between the way a word is said and the way it is spelt. Variations include different ways of spelling the same sound, the use of so-called silent letters and groups of letters in some words and, sometimes, spelling that has become separated from the way that words are now pronounced, such as the *-le* ending in *table*. Pupils' motor skills also need to be sufficiently advanced for them to write down ideas that they may be able to compose orally. In addition, writing is intrinsically harder than reading: pupils are likely to be able to read and understand more complex writing (in terms of its vocabulary and structure) than they are capable of producing themselves.

For pupils who do not have the phonic knowledge and skills they need for Year 2, teachers should use the Year 1 Programmes of Study for word reading and spelling so that pupils' word reading skills catch up. However, teachers should use the Year 2 Programme of Study for comprehension so that these pupils hear and talk about new books, poems, other writing and vocabulary with the rest of the class.

Year 2 Programme of Study (statutory requirements)	Notes and guidance (non-statutory)
READING **Word reading** Pupils should be taught to: • continue to apply phonic knowledge and skills as the route to decode words until automatic decoding has become embedded and reading is fluent • read accurately by blending the sounds in words that contain the graphemes taught so far, especially recognising alternative sounds for graphemes • read accurately words of two or more syllables that contain the same graphemes as above • read words containing common suffixes • read further common exception words, noting unusual correspondence between spelling and sound and where these occur in the word • read most words quickly and accurately, without overt sounding and blending, when they have been frequently encountered • read aloud books closely matched to their improving phonic knowledge, sounding out unfamiliar words accurately, automatically and without undue hesitation • re-read these books to build up their fluency and confidence in word reading.	**READING** **Word Reading** Pupils should revise and consolidate the GPCs and the common exception words taught in Year 1. The exception words taught will vary slightly, depending on the phonics programme being used. As soon as pupils can read words comprising the Year 2 GPCs accurately and speedily, they should move on to the Years 3 and 4 Programme of Study for word reading. When pupils are taught how to read longer words, they should be shown syllable boundaries and how to read each syllable seperately before they combine them to read the word. Pupils should be taught how to read suffixes by building on the root words that they have already learned. The whole suffix should be taught as well as the letters that make it up. Pupils who are still at the early stages of learning to read should have ample practice in reading books that are closely matched to their developing phonic knowledge and knowledge of common exception words. As soon as the decoding of most regular words and common exception words is embedded fully, the range of books that pupils can read independently will expand rapidly. Pupils should have opportunities to exercise choice in selecting books and be taught how to do so.

Year 2 Programme of Study (statutory requirements)	Notes and guidance (non-statutory)
READING **Comprehension** Pupils should be taught to: • develop pleasure in reading, motivation to read, vocabulary and understanding by: • listening to, discussing and expressing views about a wide range of contemporary and classic poetry, stories and non-fiction at a level beyond that at which they can read independently • discussing the sequence of events in books and how items of information are related • becoming increasingly familiar with and retelling a wider range of stories, fairy stories and traditional tales • being introduced to non-fiction books that are structured in different ways • recognising simple recurring literary language in stories and poetry • discussing and clarifying the meanings of words, linking new meanings to known vocabulary • discussing their favourite words and phrases • continuing to build up a repertoire of poems learned by heart, appreciating these and reciting some, with appropriate intonation to make the meaning clear • understand both the books that they can already read accurately and fluently and those that they listen to by: • drawing on what they already know or on background information and vocabulary provided by the teacher • checking that the text makes sense to them as they read and correcting inaccurate reading • making inferences on the basis of what is being said and done • answering and asking questions • predicting what might happen on the basis of what has been read so far	**READING** **Comprehension** Pupils should be encouraged to read all the words in a sentence and to do this accurately, so that their understanding of what they read is not hindered by imprecise decoding, for example, by reading 'place' instead of 'palace'. Pupils should monitor what they read, checking that the word they have decoded fits in with what else they have read and makes sense in the context of what they already know about the topic. The meaning of new words should be explained to pupils within the context of what they are reading, and they should be encouraged to use morphology, such as prefixes, to work out unknown words. Pupils should learn about cause and effect in both narrative and non-fiction (for example, what has prompted a character's behaviour in a story; why certain dates are commemorated annually). 'Thinking aloud' when reading to pupils may help them to understand what skilled readers do. Deliberate steps should be taken to increase pupils' vocabulary and their awareness of grammar so that they continue to understand the differences between spoken and written language. Discussion should be demonstrated to pupils. They should be guided to participate in it and they should be helped to consider the opinions of others. They should receive feedback on their discussions. Roleplay and other drama techniques can help pupils to identify with and explore characters. In these ways, they extend their understanding of what they read and have opportunities to try out the language they have listened to.

Year 2 Programme of Study (statutory requirements)

- participate in discussion about books, poems and other works that are read to them and those that they can read for themselves, taking turns and listening to what others say
- explain and discuss their understanding of books, poems and other material, both those that they listen to and those that they read for themselves.

WRITING

Transcription

Spelling (see English Appendix 1)

Pupils should be taught to:

- spell by:
  - segmenting spoken words into phonemes and representing these by graphemes, spelling many correctly
  - learning new ways of spelling phonemes for which one or more spellings are already known, and learn some words with each spelling, including a few common homophones
  - learning to spell common exception words
  - learning to spell more words with contracted forms
  - learning the possessive apostrophe (singular), for example, the girl's book
  - distinguishing between homophones and near-homophones
- add suffixes to spell longer words, eg *-ment, -ness, -ful, -less, -ly*
- apply spelling rules and guidelines, as listed in English Appendix 1
- write from memory simple sentences dictated by the teacher that include words using the GPCs, common exception words and punctuation taught so far.

Notes and guidance (non-statutory)

WRITING

Transcription

Spelling

In Year 2, pupils move towards more word-specific knowledge of spelling, including homophones. The process of spelling should be emphasised: that is, that spelling involves segmenting spoken words into phonemes and then representing all the phonemes by graphemes in the right order. Pupils should do this both for single-syllable and multi-syllabic words.

At this stage children's spelling should be phonically plausible, even if not always correct. Misspellings of words that pupils have been taught should be corrected; other misspelt words can be used as an opportunity to teach pupils about alternative ways of representing those sounds.

Pupils should be encouraged to apply their knowledge of suffixes from their word reading to their spelling. They should also draw from and apply their growing knowledge of word and spelling structure, as well as their knowledge of root words.

Year 2 Programme of Study (statutory requirements)	Notes and guidance (non-statutory)
Handwriting	**Handwriting**
Pupils should be taught to:	Pupils should revise and practise correct letter formation frequently. They should be taught to write with a joined style as soon as they can form letters securely with the correct orientation.
• form lower-case letters of the correct size relative to one another	
• start using some of the diagonal and horizontal strokes needed to join letters and understand which letters, when adjacent to one another, are best left unjoined	
• write capital letters and digits of the correct size, orientation and relationship to one another and to lower-case letters	
• use spacing between words that reflects the size of the letters.	
Composition	**Composition**
Pupils should be taught to:	Reading and listening to whole books, not simply extracts, helps pupils to increase their vocabulary and grammatical knowledge, including their knowledge of the vocabulary and grammar of Standard English. These activities also help them to understand how different types of writing, including narratives, are structured. All these can be drawn on for their writing.
• develop positive attitudes towards and stamina for writing by:	
– writing narratives about personal experiences and those of others (real and fictional)	
– writing about real events	
– writing poetry	Pupils should understand, through being shown, the skills and processes essential to writing: that is, thinking aloud as they collect ideas, drafting and re-reading to check their meaning is clear.
– writing for different purposes	
• consider what they are going to write before beginning by:	Drama and roleplay can contribute to the quality of pupils' writing by providing opportunities for pupils to develop and order their ideas by playing roles and improvising scenes in various settings.
– planning or saying out loud what they are going to write about	
– writing down ideas and/or key words, including new vocabulary	Pupils might draw on and use new vocabulary from their reading, their discussions about it (one-to-one and as a whole class) and from their wider experiences.
– encapsulating what they want to say, sentence by sentence	
• make simple additions, revisions and corrections to their own writing by:	
– evaluating their writing with the teacher and other pupils	
– re-reading to check that their writing makes sense and that verbs to indicate time are used correctly and consistently, including verbs in the continuous form	
– proofreading to check for errors in spelling, grammar and punctuation (for example, ends of sentences punctuated correctly)	
• read aloud what they have written with appropriate intonation to make the meaning clear.	

Year 2 Programme of Study (statutory requirements)	Notes and guidance (non-statutory)

Vocabulary, grammar and punctuation
 	
Pupils should be taught to:
 	
• develop their understanding of the concepts set out in English Appendix 2 by:
 	
  • learning how to use both familiar and new punctuation correctly (see English Appendix 2), including full stops, capital letters, exclamation marks, question marks, commas for lists and apostrophes for contracted forms and the possessive (singular)
 	
• learn how to use:
 	
  • sentences with different forms: statement, question, exclamation, command
 	
  • expanded noun phrases to describe and specify, for example, *the blue butterfly*
 	
  • the present and past tenses correctly and consistently including the progressive form
 	
  • subordination (using *when, if, that,* or *because*) and coordination (using *or, and,* or *but*)
 	
  • the grammar for year 2 in English Appendix 2
 	
  • some features of written Standard English
 	
• use and understand the grammatical terminology in English Appendix 2 in discussing their writing.
	Vocabulary, grammar and punctuation
	
	The terms for discussing language should be embedded for pupils in the course of discussing their writing with them. Their attention should be drawn to the technical terms they need to learn.

Lower Key Stage 2 – Years 3–4

By the beginning of Year 3, pupils should be able to read books written at an age-appropriate interest level. They should be able to read them accurately and at a speed that is sufficient for them to focus on understanding what they read rather than on decoding individual words. They should be able to decode most new words outside their spoken vocabulary, making a good approximation to the word's pronunciation. As their decoding skills become increasingly secure, teaching should be directed more towards developing their vocabulary and the breadth and depth of their reading, making sure that they become independent, fluent and enthusiastic readers who read widely and frequently. They should be developing their understanding and enjoyment of stories, poetry, plays and non-fiction, and learning to read silently. They should also be developing their knowledge and skills in reading non-fiction about a wide range of subjects. They should be learning to justify their views about what they have read: with support at the start of Year 3 and increasingly independently by the end of Year 4.

Pupils should be able to write down their ideas with a reasonable degree of accuracy and with good sentence punctuation. Teachers should therefore be consolidating pupils' writing skills, their vocabulary, their grasp of sentence structure and their knowledge of linguistic terminology. Teaching them to develop as writers involves teaching them to enhance the effectiveness of what they write as well as increasing their competence. Teachers should make sure that pupils build on what they have learned, particularly in terms of the range of their writing and the more varied grammar, vocabulary and narrative structures from which they can draw on to express their ideas. Pupils should be beginning to understand how writing can be different from speech. Joined handwriting should be the norm; pupils should be able to use it fast enough to keep pace with what they want to say. Pupils' spelling of common words should be correct, including exception words and other words that they have learned (see English Appendix 1). Pupils should spell words as accurately as possible using their phonic knowledge and other knowledge of spelling, such as morphology and etymology.

Most pupils will not need further direct teaching of word reading skills: they are able to decode unfamiliar words accurately, and need very few repeated experiences of this before the word is stored in such a way that they can read it without overt sound-blending. They should demonstrate understanding of figurative language, distinguish shades of meaning among related words and use age-appropriate, academic vocabulary. As in Key Stage 1, however, pupils who are still struggling to decode need to be taught to do this urgently through a rigorous and systematic phonics programme so that they catch up rapidly with their peers. If they cannot decode independently and fluently, they will find it increasingly difficult to understand what they read and to write down what they want to say. As far as possible, however, they should follow the Year 3 and 4 Programme of Study in terms of listening to new books, hearing and learning new vocabulary and grammatical structures, and discussing these.

Specific requirements for pupils to discuss what they are learning and to develop their wider skills in spoken language form part of this Programme of Study. In Years 3 and 4, pupils should become more familiar with and confident in using language in a greater variety of situations, for a variety of audiences and purposes, including through drama, formal presentations and debate.

Years 3–4 Programme of Study (statutory requirements)	Notes and guidance (non-statutory)
READING	**READING**
Word reading	**Word reading**
Pupils should be taught to:	At this stage, teaching comprehension should be taking precedence over teaching word reading directly. Any focus on word reading should support the development of vocabulary.
• apply their growing knowledge of root words, prefixes and suffixes (etymology and morphology) as listed in English Appendix 1, both to read aloud and to understand the meaning of new words they meet	When pupils are taught to read longer words, they should be supported to test out different pronunciations. They will attempt to match what they decode to words they may have already heard but may not have seen in print: for example, in reading *technical*, the pronunciation /tɛtʃnɪkəl/ ('technical') might not sound familiar, but /tɛknɪkəl/ ('teknical') should.
• read further exception words, noting the unusual correspondences between spelling and sound, and where these occur in the word.	

Years 3–4 Programme of Study (statutory requirements)

READING

Comprehension

Pupils should be taught to:

- develop positive attitudes to reading and understanding of what they read by:

  - listening to and discussing a wide range of fiction, poetry, plays, non-fiction and reference books or textbooks

  - reading books that are structured in different ways and reading for a range of purposes

  - using dictionaries to check the meaning of words that they have read

  - increasing their familiarity with a wide range of books, including fairy stories, myths and legends, and retelling some of these orally

  - identifying themes and conventions in a wide range of books

  - preparing poems and play scripts to read aloud and to perform, showing understanding through intonation, tone, volume and action

  - discussing words and phrases that capture the reader's interest and imagination

  - recognising some different forms of poetry (for example, free verse, narrative poetry)

- understand what they read, in books they can read independently, by:

  - checking that the text makes sense to them, discussing their understanding and explaining the meaning of words in context

  - asking questions to improve their understanding of a text

  - drawing inferences such as inferring characters' feelings, thoughts and motives from their actions, and justifying inferences with evidence

  - predicting what might happen from details stated and implied

Notes and guidance (non-statutory)

READING

Comprehension

The focus should continue to be on pupils' comprehension as a primary element in reading. The knowledge and skills that pupils need in order to comprehend are very similar at different ages. This is why the Programmes of Study for comprehension in Years 3 and 4 and Years 5 and 6 are similar: the complexity of the writing increases the level of challenge.

Pupils should be taught to recognise themes in what they read, such as the triumph of good over evil or the use of magical devices in fairy stories and folk tales.

They should also learn the conventions of different types of writing, (for example, the greeting in letters, a diary written in the first person or the use of presentational devices such as numbering and headings in instructions).

Pupils should be taught to use the skills they have learned earlier and continue to apply these skills to read for different reasons, including for pleasure, or to find out information and the meaning of new words.

Pupils should continue to have opportunities to listen frequently to stories, poems, non-fiction and other writing, including whole books and not just extracts, so that they build on what was taught previously. In this way, they also meet books and authors that they might not choose themselves. Pupils should also have opportunities to exercise choice in selecting books and be taught how to do so, with teachers making use of any available library services and expertise to support this.

Years 3–4 Programme of Study (statutory requirements)	Notes and guidance (non-statutory)
• identifying main ideas drawn from more than one paragraph and summarising these • identifying how language, structure, and presentation contribute to meaning • retrieve and record information from non-fiction • participate in discussion about both books that are read to them and those they can read for themselves, taking turns and listening to what others say.	Reading, re-reading and rehearsing poems and plays for presentation and performance give pupils opportunities to discuss language, including vocabulary, extending their interest in the meaning and origin of words. Pupils should be encouraged to use drama approaches to understand how to perform plays and poems to support their understanding of the meaning. These activities also provide them with an incentive to find out what expression is required, so feeding into comprehension. In using non-fiction, pupils should know what information they need to look for before they begin and be clear about the task. They should be shown how to use contents pages and indexes to locate information. Pupils should have guidance about the kinds of explanations and questions that are expected from them. They should help to develop, agree on, and evaluate rules for effective discussion. The expectation should be that all pupils take part.
WRITING **Transcription** *Spelling* (see English Appendix 1) Pupils should be taught to: • use further prefixes and suffixes and understand how to add them (English Appendix 1) • spell further homophones • spell words that are often misspelt (English Appendix 1) • place the possessive apostrophe accurately in words with regular plurals (for example, girls', boys') and in words with irregular plurals (for example, children's) • use the first two or three letters of a word to check its spelling in a dictionary • write from memory simple sentences, dictated by the teacher, that include words and punctuation taught so far.	**WRITING** **Transcription** *Spelling* Pupils should learn to spell new words correctly and have plenty of practice in spelling them. As in Years 1 and 2, pupils should continue to be supported in understanding and applying the concepts of word structure (see English Appendix 2). Pupils need sufficient knowledge of spelling in order to use dictionaries efficiently.

Years 3–4 Programme of Study (statutory requirements)

Handwriting

Pupils should be taught to:

- use the diagonal and horizontal strokes that are needed to join letters and understand which letters, when adjacent to one another, are best left unjoined

- increase the legibility, consistency and quality of their handwriting, for example by ensuring that the downstrokes of letters are parallel and equidistant; that lines of writing are spaced sufficiently so that the ascenders and descenders of letters do not touch.

Composition

Pupils should be taught to:

- plan their writing by:
  - discussing writing similar to that which they are planning to write in order to understand and learn from its structure, vocabulary and grammar
  - discussing and recording ideas
- draft and write by:
  - composing and rehearsing sentences orally (including dialogue), progressively building a varied and rich vocabulary and an increasing range of sentence structures (English Appendix 2)
  - organising paragraphs around a theme
  - in narratives, creating settings, characters and plot
  - in non-narrative material, using simple organisational devices for example, headings and subheadings
- evaluate and edit by:
  - assessing the effectiveness of their own and others' writing and suggesting improvements
  - proposing changes to grammar and vocabulary to improve consistency, including the accurate use of pronouns in sentences
- proofread for spelling and punctuation errors
- read aloud their own writing, to a group or the whole class, using appropriate intonation and controlling the tone and volume so that the meaning is clear.

Notes and guidance (non-statutory)

Handwriting

Pupils should be using joined handwriting throughout their independent writing. Handwriting should continue to be taught, with the aim of increasing the fluency with which pupils are able to write down what they want to say. This, in turn, will support their composition and spelling.

Composition

Pupils should continue to have opportunities to write for a range of real purposes and audiences as part of their work across the curriculum. These purposes and audiences should underpin the decisions about the form the writing should take, such as a narrative, an explanation or a description.

Pupils should understand, through being shown these, the skills and processes that are essential for writing: that is, thinking aloud to explore and collect ideas, drafting, and re-reading to check their meaning is clear, including doing so as the writing develops. Pupils should be taught to monitor whether their own writing makes sense in the same way that they monitor their reading, checking at different levels.

Years 3–4 Programme of Study (statutory requirements)	Notes and guidance (non-statutory)

Vocabulary, grammar and punctuation
 	
Pupils should be taught to:
 	
• develop their understanding of the concepts set out in English Appendix 2 by:
 	
    • extending the range of sentences with more than one clause by using a wider range of conjunctions, including *when, if, because, although*
 	
    • using the present perfect form of verbs in contrast to the past tense
 	
    • choosing nouns or pronouns appropriately for clarity and cohesion and to avoid repetition
 	
    • using conjunctions, adverbs and prepositions to express time and cause
 	
    • using fronted adverbials
 	
    • learning the grammar for years 3 and 4 in English Appendix 2
 	
• indicate grammatical and other features by:
 	
    • using commas after fronted adverbials
 	
    • indicating possession by using the possessive apostrophe with plural nouns
 	
    • using and punctuating direct speech
 	
• use and understand the grammatical terminology in English Appendix 2 accurately and appropriately when discussing their writing and reading.
	Vocabulary, grammar and punctuation
	
	Grammar should be taught explicitly: pupils should be taught the terminology and concepts set out in English Appendix 2, and be able to apply them correctly to examples of real language, such as their own writing or books that they have read.
	
	At this stage, pupils should start to learn about some of the differences between Standard English and non-Standard English and begin to apply what they have learned, for example, in writing dialogue for characters.

Upper Key Stage 2 – Years 5–6

By the beginning of Year 5, pupils should be able to read aloud a wider range of poetry and books written at an age-appropriate interest level with accuracy and at a reasonable speaking pace. They should be able to read most words effortlessly and to work out how to pronounce unfamiliar written words with increasing automaticity. If the pronunciation sounds unfamiliar, they should ask for help in determining both the meaning of the word and how to pronounce it correctly.

They should be able to prepare readings, with appropriate intonation to show their understanding, and should be able to summarise and present a familiar story in their own words. They should be reading widely and frequently, outside as well as in school, for pleasure and information. They should be able to read silently, and then discuss what they have read.

Pupils should be able to write down their ideas quickly. Their grammar and punctuation should be broadly accurate. Pupils' spelling of most words taught so far should be accurate and they should be able to spell words that they have not yet been taught by using what they have learned about how spelling works in English.

During Years 5 and 6, teachers should continue to emphasise pupils' enjoyment and understanding of language, especially vocabulary, to support their reading and writing. Pupils' knowledge of language, gained from stories, plays, poetry, non-fiction and textbooks, will support their increasing fluency as readers, their facility as writers, and their comprehension. As in Years 3 and 4, pupils should be taught to enhance the effectiveness of their writing as well as their competence.

It is essential that pupils whose decoding skills are poor are taught through a rigorous and systematic phonics programme so that they catch up rapidly with their peers in terms of their decoding and spelling. However, as far as possible, these pupils should follow the upper Key Stage 2 Programme of Study in terms of listening to books and other writing that they have not come across before, hearing and learning new vocabulary and grammatical structures, and having a chance to talk about all of these.

By the end of Year 6, pupils' reading and writing should be sufficiently fluent and effortless for them to manage the general demands of the curriculum in Year 7, across all subjects and not just in English, but there will continue to be a need for pupils to learn subject-specific vocabulary. They should be able to reflect their understanding of the audience for and purpose of their writing by selecting appropriate vocabulary and grammar. Teachers should prepare pupils for secondary education by ensuring that they can consciously control the structure of sentences in their writing and understand why sentences are constructed as they are. This involves consolidation, practice and discussion of language.

Specific requirements for pupils to discuss what they are learning and to develop their wider skills in spoken language form part of this Programme of Study. In Years 5 and 6, pupils' confidence, enjoyment and mastery of language should be extended through public speaking, performance and debate.

Years 5–6 Programme of Study (statutory requirements)

READING

Word reading

Pupils should be taught to:

- apply their growing knowledge of root words, prefixes and suffixes (morphology and etymology), as listed in English Appendix 1, both to read aloud and to understand the meaning of new words that they meet.

Notes and guidance (non-statutory)

READING

Word reading

At this stage, there should be no need for further direct teaching of word reading skills for almost all pupils. If pupils are struggling or failing in this, the reasons for this should be investigated. It is imperative that pupils are taught to read during their last two years at primary school if they enter Year 5 not being able to do so.

Pupils should be encouraged to work out any unfamiliar word. They should focus on all the letters in a word so that they do not, for example, read 'invitation' for 'imitation' simply because they might be more familiar with the first word. Accurate reading of individual words, which might be key to the meaning of a sentence or paragraph, improves comprehension.

When teachers are reading with or to pupils, attention should be paid to new vocabulary – both a word's meaning(s) and its correct pronunciation.

SCHOLASTIC

Years 5–6 Programme of Study (statutory requirements)	Notes and guidance (non-statutory)
READING	**READING**
Comprehension	**Comprehension**
Pupils should be taught to:	Even though pupils can now read independently, reading aloud to them should include whole books so that they meet books and authors that they might not choose to read themselves.
• maintain positive attitudes to reading and understanding of what they read by:	The knowledge and skills that pupils need in order to comprehend are very similar at different ages. Pupils should continue to apply what they have already learned to more complex writing.
• continuing to read and discuss an increasingly wide range of fiction, poetry, plays, non-fiction and reference books or textbooks	Pupils should be taught to recognise themes in what they read, such as loss or heroism. They should have opportunities to compare characters, consider different accounts of the same event and discuss viewpoints (both of authors and of fictional characters), within a text and across more than one text.
• reading books that are structured in different ways and reading for a range of purposes	They should continue to learn the conventions of different types of writing, such as the use of the first person in writing diaries and autobiographies.
• increasing their familiarity with a wide range of books, including myths, legends and traditional stories, modern fiction, fiction from our literary heritage, and books from other cultures and traditions	Pupils should be taught the technical and other terms needed for discussing what they hear and read, such as *metaphor, simile, analogy, imagery, style and effect.*
• recommending books that they have read to their peers, giving reasons for their choices	In using reference books, pupils need to know what information they need to look for before they begin and need to understand the task. They should be shown how to use contents pages and indexes to locate information.
• identifying and discussing themes and conventions in and across a wide range of writing	The skills of information retrieval that are taught should be applied, for example, in reading history, geography and science textbooks, and in contexts where pupils are genuinely motivated to find out information, for example, reading information leaflets before a gallery or museum visit or reading a theatre programme or review. Teachers should consider making use of any available library services and expertise to support this.
• making comparisons within and across books	Pupils should have guidance about and feedback on the quality of their explanations and contributions to discussions.
• learning a wider range of poetry by heart	
• preparing poems and plays to read aloud and to perform, showing understanding through intonation, tone and volume so that the meaning is clear to an audience	
• understand what they read by:	
• checking that the book makes sense to them, discussing their understanding and exploring the meaning of words in context	
• asking questions to improve their understanding	
• drawing inferences such as inferring characters' feelings, thoughts and motives from their actions, and justifying inferences with evidence	
• predicting what might happen from details stated and implied	
• summarising the main ideas drawn from more than one paragraph, identifying key details that support the main ideas	

Years 5–6 Programme of Study (statutory requirements)	Notes and guidance (non-statutory)
• identifying how language, structure and presentation contribute to meaning • discuss and evaluate how authors use language, including figurative language, considering the impact on the reader • distinguish between statements of fact and opinion • retrieve, record and present information from non-fiction • participate in discussions about books that are read to them and those they can read for themselves, building on their own and others' ideas and challenging views courteously • explain and discuss their understanding of what they have read, including through formal presentations and debates, maintaining a focus on the topic and using notes where necessary • provide reasoned justifications for their views.	Pupils should be shown how to compare characters, settings, themes and other aspects of what they read.
WRITING **Transcription** *Spelling* (see English Appendix 1) Pupils should be taught to: • use further prefixes and suffixes and understand the guidelines for adding them • spell some words with 'silent' letters, for example, *knight, psalm, solemn* • continue to distinguish between homophones and other words which are often confused • use knowledge of morphology and etymology in spelling and understand that the spelling of some words needs to be learned specifically, as listed in English Appendix 1 • use dictionaries to check the spelling and meaning of words • use the first three or four letters of a word to check spelling, meaning or both of these in a dictionary • use a thesaurus.	**WRITING** **Transcription** *Spelling* As in earlier years, pupils should continue to be taught to understand and apply the concepts of word structure so that they can draw on their knowledge of morphology and etymology to spell correctly.

Years 5–6 Programme of Study (statutory requirements)	Notes and guidance (non-statutory)

Handwriting and presentation
 	
Pupils should be taught to:
 	
• write legibly, fluently and with increasing speed by:
 	
  • choosing which shape of a letter to use when given choices and deciding, as part of their personal style, whether or not to join specific letters
 	
  • choosing the writing implement that is best suited for a task
	Handwriting and presentation
	
	Pupils should continue to practise handwriting and be encouraged to increase the speed of it, so that problems with forming letters do not get in the way of their writing down what they want to say. They should be clear about what standard of handwriting is appropriate for a particular task, for example, quick notes or a final handwritten version. They should also be taught to use an unjoined style, for example, for labelling a diagram or data, writing an email address, or for algebra and capital letters for example, for filling in a form.

Composition
 	
Pupils should be taught to:
 	
• plan their writing by:
 	
  • identifying the audience for and purpose of the writing, selecting the appropriate form and using other similar writing as models for their own
 	
  • noting and developing initial ideas, drawing on reading and research where necessary
 	
  • in writing narratives, considering how authors have developed characters and settings in what they have read, listened to or seen performed
 	
• draft and write by:
 	
  • selecting appropriate grammar and vocabulary, understanding how such choices can change and enhance meaning
 	
  • in narratives, describing settings, characters and atmosphere and integrating dialogue to convey character and advance the action
 	
  • précising longer passages
 	
  • using a wide range of devices to build cohesion within and across paragraphs
 	
  • using further organisational and presentational devices to structure text and to guide the reader (for example, headings, bullet points, underlining)
	Composition
	
	Pupils should understand, through being shown, the skills and processes essential for writing: that is, thinking aloud to generate ideas, drafting and re-reading to check that the meaning is clear.

Years 5–6 Programme of Study (statutory requirements)	Notes and guidance (non-statutory)

• evaluate and edit by:
 	
  • assessing the effectiveness of their own and others' writing
 	
  • proposing changes to vocabulary, grammar and punctuation to enhance effects and clarify meaning
 	
  • ensuring the consistent and correct use of tense throughout a piece of writing
 	
  • ensuring correct subject and verb agreement when using singular and plural, distinguishing between the language of speech and writing and choosing the appropriate register
 	
• proofread for spelling and punctuation errors
 	
• perform their own compositions, using appropriate intonation, volume and movement so that meaning is clear.	

Years 5–6 Programme of Study (statutory requirements)

Vocabulary, grammar and punctuation

Pupils should be taught to:

- develop their understanding of the concepts set out in English Appendix 2 by:

  - recognising vocabulary and structures that are appropriate for formal speech and writing, including subjunctive forms

  - using passive verbs to affect the presentation of information in a sentence

  - using the perfect form of verbs to mark relationships of time and cause

  - using expanded noun phrases to convey complicated information concisely

  - using modal verbs or adverbs to indicate degrees of possibility

  - using relative clauses beginning with *who, which, where, when, whose, that* or with an implied (ie omitted) relative pronoun

  - learning the grammar for years 5–6 in English Appendix 2

- indicate grammatical and other features by:

  - using commas to clarify meaning or avoid ambiguity in writing

  - using hyphens to avoid ambiguity

  - using brackets, dashes or commas to indicate parenthesis

  - using semi-colons, colons or dashes to mark boundaries between independent clauses

  - using a colon to introduce a list

  - punctuating bullet points consistently

- use and understand the grammatical terminology in English Appendix 2 accurately and appropriately in discussing their writing and reading.

Notes and guidance (non-statutory)

Vocabulary, grammar and punctuation

Pupils should continue to add to their knowledge of linguistic terms, including those to describe grammar, so that they can discuss their writing and reading.

English Appendix 1: Spelling

Most people read words more accurately than they spell them. The younger pupils are, the truer this is.

By the end of Year 1, pupils should be able to read a large number of different words containing the GPCs that they have learned, whether or not they have seen these words before. Spelling, however, is a very different matter. Once pupils have learned more than one way of spelling particular sounds, choosing the right letter or letters depends on their either having made a conscious effort to learn the words or having absorbed them less consciously through their reading. Younger pupils have not had enough time to learn or absorb the accurate spelling of all the words that they may want to write.

This appendix provides examples of words embodying each pattern which is taught. Many of the words listed as 'example words' for Years 1 and 2, including almost all those listed as 'exception words', are used frequently in pupils' writing, and therefore it is worth pupils learning the correct spelling. The 'exception words' contain GPCs which have not yet been taught as widely applicable, but this may be because they are applicable in very few age-appropriate words rather than because they are rare in English words in general.

The wordlists for Years 3 and 4 and Years 5 and 6 are statutory. The lists are a mixture both of words pupils frequently use in their writing and those which they often misspell. Some of the listed words may be thought of as quite challenging, but the 100 words in each list can be covered in fewer than two school years if teachers simply add words each week.

The rules and guidance are intended to support the teaching of spelling. Phonic knowledge should continue to underpin spelling after Key Stage 1; teachers should still draw pupils' attention to GPCs that do and do not fit in with what has been taught so far. Increasingly, however, pupils also need to understand the role of morphology and etymology. Although particular GPCs in root words simply have to be learned, teachers can help pupils to understand relationships between meaning and spelling where these are relevant. For example, understanding the relationship between medical and medicine may help pupils to spell the /s/ sound in medicine with the letter 'c'. Pupils can also be helped to spell words with prefixes and suffixes correctly if they understand some general principles for adding them. Teachers should be familiar with what pupils have been taught about spelling in earlier years, such as which rules pupils have been taught for adding prefixes and suffixes.

In this spelling appendix, the left-hand column is statutory; the middle and right-hand columns are non-statutory guidance.

The International Phonetic Alphabet (IPA) is used to represent sounds (phonemes). A table showing the IPA is provided in this document.

Year 1

Spelling – work for Year 1

Statutory requirements

Statutory requirements	Rules and guidance (non-statutory)	Example words (non-statutory)
Revision of Reception work The boundary between revision of work covered in Reception and the introduction of new work may vary according to the programme used, but basic revision should include: • all letters of the alphabet and the sounds which they most commonly represent • consonant digraphs which have been taught and the sounds which they represent • vowel digraphs which have been taught and the sounds which they represent • the process of segmenting spoken words into sounds before choosing graphemes to represent the sounds • words with adjacent consonants • guidance and rules which have been taught		
The sounds /f/, /l/, /s/, /z/ and /k/ spelt ff, ll, ss, zz and ck	The /f/, /l/, /s/, /z/ and /k/ sounds are usually spelt as **ff, ll, ss, zz** and **ck** if they come straight after a single vowel letter in short words. **Exceptions:** *if, pal, us, bus, yes.*	off, well, miss, buzz, back
The /ŋ/ sound spelt n before k		bank, think, honk, sunk
Division of words into syllables	Each syllable is like a 'beat' in the spoken word. Words of more than one syllable often have an unstressed syllable in which the vowel sound is unclear.	pocket, rabbit, carrot, thunder, sunset
-tch	The /tʃ/ sound is usually spelt as **tch** if it comes straight after a single vowel letter. **Exceptions:** *rich, which, much, such.*	catch, fetch, kitchen, notch, hutch

The /v/ sound at the end of words	English words hardly ever end with the letter **v**, so if a word ends with a /v/ sound, the letter **e** usually needs to be added after the 'v'.	have, live, give
Adding s and es to words (plural of nouns and the third person singular of verbs)	If the ending sounds like /s/ or /z/, it is spelt as -s. If the ending sounds like /ɪz/ and forms an extra syllable or 'beat' in the word, it is spelt as **-es**.	cats, dogs, spends, rocks, thanks, catches
Adding the endings -ing, -ed and -er to verbs where no change is needed to the root word	**-ing** and **-er** always add an extra syllable to the word and **-ed** sometimes does. The past tense of some verbs may sound as if it ends in /ɪd/ (extra syllable), /d/ or /t/ (no extra syllable), but all these endings are spelt **-ed**. If the verb ends in two consonant letters (the same or different), the ending is simply added on.	hunting, hunted, hunter, buzzing, buzzed, buzzer, jumping, jumped, jumper
Adding -er and -est to adjectives where no change is needed to the root word	As with verbs (see above), if the adjective ends in two consonant letters (the same or different), the ending is simply added on.	grander, grandest, fresher, freshest, quicker, quickest
Vowel digraphs and trigraphs	Some may already be known, depending on the programmes used in reception, but some will be new.	
ai oi	The digraphs ai and oi are virtually never used at the end of English words.	rain, wait, train, paid, afraid oil, join, coin, point, soil
ay oy	**ay** and **oy** are used for those sounds at the end of words and at the end of syllables.	day, play, say, way, stay boy, toy, enjoy, annoy
a–e		made, came, same, take, safe
e–e		these, theme, complete
i–e		five, ride, like, time, side
o–e		home, those, woke, hope, hole
u–e	Both the /u:/ and /ju:/ ('oo' and 'yoo') sounds can be spelt as **u–e**.	June, rule, rude, use, tube, tune
ar		car, start, park, arm, garden
ee		see, tree, green, meet, week
ea (/iː/)		sea, dream, meat, each, read (present tense)
ea (/ɛ/)		head, bread, meant, instead, read (past tense)
er (/ɜː/)		(stressed sound): her, term, verb, person
er (/ə/)		(unstressed schwa sound): better, under, summer, winter, sister
ir		girl, bird, shirt, first, third
ur		turn, hurt, church, burst, Thursday

Pattern	Rule	Examples
oo (/uː/)	Very few words end with the letters **oo**, although the few that do are often words that primary children in year 1 will encounter, for example, *zoo*	food, pool, The Moon, zoo, soon
oo (/ʊ/)		book, took, foot, wood, good
oa	The digraph **oa** is rare at the end of an English word.	boat, coat, road, coach, goal
oe		toe, goes
ou	The only common English word ending in **ou** is *you*.	out, about, mouth, around, sound
ow (/aʊ/) ow (/əʊ/) ue ew	Both the /uː/ and /juː/ ('oo' and 'yoo') sounds can be spelt as **u–e**, **ue** and **ew**. If words end in the /oo/ sound, **ue** and **ew** are more common spellings than **oo**.	now, how, brown, down, town / own, blow, snow, grow, show / blue, clue, true, rescue, Tuesday / new, few, grew, flew, drew, threw
ie (/aɪ/)		lie, tie, pie, cried, tried, dried
ie (/iː/)		chief, field, thief
igh		high, night, light, bright, right
or		for, short, born, horse, morning
ore		more, score, before, wore, shore
aw		saw, draw, yawn, crawl
au		author, August, dinosaur, astronaut
air		air, fair, pair, hair, chair
ear		dear, hear, beard, near, year
ear (/ɛə/)		bear, pear, wear
are (/ɛə/)		bare, dare, care, share, scared
Words ending -y (/iː/ or /ɪ/)		very, happy, funny, party, family
New consonant spellings ph and wh	The /f/ sound is not usually spelt as **ph** in short everyday words (eg *fat, fill, fun*).	dolphin, alphabet, phonics, elephant when, where, which, wheel, while
Using k for the /k/ sound	The /k/ sound is spelt as **k** rather than as c before **e**, **i** and **y**.	Kent, sketch, kit, skin, frisky
Adding the prefix un-	The prefix **un-** is added to the beginning of a word without any change to the spelling of the root word.	unhappy, undo, unload, unfair, unlock
Compound words	Compound words are two words joined together. Each part of the longer word is spelt as it would be if it were on its own.	football, playground, farmyard, bedroom, blackberry
Common exception words	Pupils' attention should be drawn to the grapheme-phoneme correspondences that do and do not fit in with what has been taught so far.	the, a, do, to, today, of, said, says, are, were, was, is, his, has, I, you, your, they, be, he, me, she, we, no, go, so, by, my, here, there, where, love, come, some, one, once, ask, friend, school, put, push, pull, full, house, our – and/or others, according to the programme used.

Year 2

Spelling - revision of work from Year 1	As words with new GPCs are introduced, many previously-taught GPCs can be revised at the same time as these words will usually contain them.	
Spelling - new work for Year 2		
Statutory requirements	**Rules and guidance (non-statutory)**	**Example words (non-statutory)**
The /dʒ/ sound spelt as ge and dge at the end of words, and sometimes spelt as g elsewhere in words before e, i and y	The letter j is never used for the /dʒ/ ("dge") sound at the end of English words. At the end of a word, the /dʒ/ sound is spelt -**dge** straight after the /æ/, /ɛ/, /ɪ/, /ɒ/, /ʌ/ and /ʊ/ sounds (sometimes called 'short' vowels).	badge, edge, bridge, dodge, fudge
	After all other sounds, whether vowels or consonants, the /dʒ/ sound is spelt as -**ge** at the end of a word. In other positions in words, the /dʒ/ sound is often (but not always) spelt as g before e, i, and y. The /dʒ/ sound is always spelt as j before a, o and u.	age, huge, change, charge, bulge, village gem, giant, magic, giraffe, energy

jacket, jar, jog, join, adjust |
The /s/ sound spelt c before e, i and y		race, ice, cell, city, fancy
The /n/ sound spelt kn and (less often) gn at the beginning of words	The 'k' and 'g' at the beginning of these words was sounded hundreds of years ago.	knock, know, knee, gnat, gnaw
The /r/ sound spelt wr at the beginning of words	This spelling probably also reflects an old pronunciation.	write, written, wrote, wrong, wrap
The /l/ or /əl/ sound spelt -le at the end of words	The -**le** spelling is the most common spelling for this sound at the end of words.	table, apple, bottle, little, middle
The /l/ or /əl/ sound spelt -el at the end of words	The -**el** spelling is much less common than -**le**. The -**el** spelling is used after **m, n, r, s, v, w** and more often than not after **s**.	camel, tunnel, squirrel, travel, towel, tinsel
The /l/ or /əl/ sound spelt -al at the end of words	Not many nouns end in -**al**, but many adjectives do.	metal, pedal, capital, hospital, animal
Words ending -il	There are not many of these words.	pencil, fossil, nostril
The /aɪ/ sound spelt -y at the end of words	This is by far the most common spelling for this sound at the end of words.	cry, fly, dry, try, reply, July
Adding -es to nouns and verbs ending in -y	The **y** is changed to i before -**es** is added.	flies, tries, replies, copies, babies, carries
Adding -ed, -ing, -er and -est to a root word ending in -y with a consonant before it.	The **y** is changed to i before -**ed**, -**er** and -**est** are added, but not before -**ing** as this would result in ii. The only ordinary words with **ii** are *skiing* and *taxiing*.	copied, copier, happier, happiest, cried, replied ...**but** copying, crying, replying

Rule	Description	Examples
Adding the endings -ing, -ed, -er, -est and -y to words ending in -e with a consonant before it	The -e at the end of the root word is dropped before -ing, -ed, -er, -est, -y or any other suffix beginning with a vowel letter is added. The exception is *being*.	hiking, hiked, hiker, nicer, nicest, shiny
Adding -ing, -ed, -er, -est and -y to words of one syllable ending in a single consonant letter after a single vowel letter	The last consonant letter of the root word is doubled to keep the /æ/, /ɛ/, /ɪ/, /ɒ/ and /ʌ/ sound (ie to keep the vowel 'short'). **Exception:** The letter 'x' is never doubled: *mixing, mixed, boxer, sixes*.	patting, patted, humming, hummed, dropping, dropped, sadder, saddest, fatter, fattest, runner, runny
The /ɔː/ sound spelt a before l and ll	The /ɔː/ sound ("or") is usually spelt as **a** before **l** and **ll**.	all, ball, call, walk, talk, always
The /ʌ/ sound spelt o		other, mother, brother, nothing, Monday
The /iː/ sound spelt -ey	The plural of these words is formed by the addition of -**s** (*donkeys, monkeys*, etc).	key, donkey, monkey, chimney, valley
The /ɒ/ sound spelt a after w and qu	**a** is the most common spelling for the /ɒ/ ('h**o**t') sound after **w** and **qu**.	want, watch, wander, quantity, squash
The /ɜː/ sound spelt or after w	There are not many of these words.	word, work, worm, world, worth
The /ɔː/ sound spelt ar after w	There are not many of these words.	war, warm, towards
The /ʒ/ sound spelt s		television, treasure, usual
The suffixes -ment, -ness, -ful, -less and -ly	If a suffix starts with a consonant letter, it is added straight on to most root words without any change to the last letter of those words. **Exceptions:** (1) *argument* (2) root words ending in -**y** with a consonant before it but only if the root word has more than one syllable.	enjoyment, sadness, careful, playful, hopeless, plainness (plain + ness), badly, merriment, happiness, plentiful, penniless, happily
Contractions	In contractions, the apostrophe shows where a letter or letters would be if the words were written in full (eg *can't* – *cannot*). *It's* means it is (eg *It's raining*) or sometimes *it has* (eg *It's been raining*), but *it's* is never used for the possessive.	can't, didn't, hasn't, couldn't, it's, I'll
The possessive apostrophe (singular nouns)		Megan's, Ravi's, the girl's, the child's, the man's
Words ending in -tion		station, fiction, motion, national, section
Homophones and near-homophones	It is important to know the difference in meaning between homophones.	there/their/they're, here/hear, quite/quiet, see/sea, bare/bear, one/won, sun/son, to/too/two, be/bee, blue/blew, night/knight

SCHOLASTIC

| Common exception words | Some words are exceptions in some accents but not in others – eg *past, last, fast, path* and *bath* are not exceptions in accents where the **a** in these words is pronounced /æ/, as in *cat*.

Great, break and *steak* are the only common words where the /eɪ/ sound is spelt **ea**. | door, floor, poor, because, find, kind, mind, behind, child, children*, wild, climb, most, only, both, old, cold, gold, hold, told, every, everybody, even, great, break, steak, pretty, beautiful, after, fast, last, past, father, class, grass, pass, plant, path, bath, hour, move, prove, improve, sure, sugar, eye, could, should, would, who, whole, any, many, clothes, busy, people, water, again, half, money, Mr, Mrs, parents, Christmas – and/or others according to programme used.

* Note: 'children' is not an exception to what has been taught so far but is included because of its relationship with 'child'. |

Years 3 and 4

Spelling - revision of work from Years 1 and 2	Pay special attention to the rules for adding suffixes.	
Spelling - new work for Years 3 and 4		
Statutory requirements	**Rules and guidance (non-statutory)**	**Example words (non-statutory)**
Adding suffixes beginning with vowel letters to words of more than one syllable	If the last syllable of a word is stressed and ends with one consonant letter which has just one vowel letter before it, the final consonant letter is doubled before any ending beginning with a vowel letter is added. The consonant letter is not doubled if the syllable is unstressed.	forgetting, forgotten, beginning, beginner, prefer, preferred

gardening, gardener, limiting, limited, limitation |
| **The /ɪ/ sound spelt y elsewhere than at the end of words** | These words should be learned as needed. | myth, gym, Egypt, pyramid, mystery |
| **The /ʌ/ sound spelt ou** | These words should be learned as needed. | young, touch, double, trouble, country |
| **More prefixes** | Most prefixes are added to the beginning of root words without any changes in spelling, but see **in-** below. Like **un-**, the prefixes **dis-** and **mis-** have negative meanings. The prefix **in-** can mean both 'not' and 'in'/'into'. In the words given here it means 'not'. Before a root word starting with **l**, **in-** becomes **il**. Before a root word starting with **m** or **p**, **in-** becomes **im-**. Before a root word starting with **r**, **in-** becomes **ir-**. **re-** means 'again' or 'back'. **sub-** means 'under'. **inter-** means 'between' or 'among'.

super- means 'above'. **anti-** means 'against'. **auto-** means 'self' or 'own'. | **dis-, mis-**: disappoint, disagree, disobey misbehave, mislead, misspell (mis + spell) **in-**: inactive, incorrect

illegal, illegible immature, immortal, impossible, impatient, imperfect irregular, irrelevant, irresponsible **re-**: redo, refresh, return, reappear, redecorate **sub-**: subdivide, subheading, submarine, submerge **inter-**: interact, intercity, international, interrelated (inter + related) **super-**: supermarket, superman, superstar **anti-**: antiseptic, anti-clockwise, antisocial **auto-**: autobiography, autograph |
| **The suffix -ation** | The suffix **-ation** is added to verbs to form nouns. The rules already learned still apply. | information, adoration, sensation, preparation, admiration |
| **The suffix -ly** | The suffix **-ly** is added to an adjective to form an adverb. The rules already learned still apply. The suffix **-ly** starts with a consonant letter, so it is added straight on to most root words. | sadly, completely, usually (usual + ly), finally (final + ly), comically (comical + ly) |

Rule	Guidance	Examples
The suffix -ly	**Exceptions:** (1) If the root word ends in **-y** with a consonant letter before it, the **y** is changed to **i**, but only if the root word has more than one syllable. (2) If the root word ends with **-le**, the **-le** is changed to **-ly**. (3) If the root word ends with **-ic**, **-ally** is added rather than just **-ly**, except in the word *publicly*. (4) The words *truly, duly, wholly*.	happily, angrily gently, simply, humbly, nobly basically, frantically, dramatically
Words with endings sounding like /ʒə/ or /tʃə/	The ending sounding like /ʒə/ is always spelt **-sure**. The ending sounding like /tʃə/ is often spelt **-ture**, but check that the word is not a root word ending in **(t)ch** with an **er** ending – eg *teacher, catcher, richer, stretcher.*	measure, treasure, pleasure, enclosure creature, furniture, picture, nature, adventure
Endings which sound like /ʒən/	If the ending sounds like /ʒən/, it is spelt as **-sion**	division, invasion, confusion, decision, collision, television
The suffix -ous	Sometimes the root word is obvious and the usual rules apply for adding suffixes beginning with vowel letters. Sometimes there is no obvious root word. **-our** is changed to **-or** before **-ous** is added. A final 'e' must be kept if the /dʒ/ sound of 'g' is to be kept. If there is an /i:/ sound before the **-ous** ending, it is usually spelt as **i**, but a few words have **e**.	poisonous, dangerous, mountainous, famous, various tremendous, enormous, jealous humorous, glamorous, vigorous courageous, outrageous serious, obvious, curious hideous, spontaneous, courteous
Endings which sound like /ʃən/, spelt -tion, -sion, -ssion, -cian	Strictly speaking, the suffixes are **-ion** and **-cian**. Clues about whether to put **t**, **s**, **ss** or **c** before these suffixes often come from the last letter or letters of the root word. **-tion** is the most common spelling. It is used if the root word ends in **t** or **te**. **-ssion** is used if the root word ends in **ss** or **-mit**. **-sion** is used if the root word ends in **d** or **se**. **Exceptions:** *attend – attention, intend – intention.* **-cian** is used if the root word ends in **c** or **cs**.	invention, injection, action, hesitation, completion expression, discussion, confession, permission, admission expansion, extension, comprehension, tension musician, electrician, magician, politician, mathematician
Words with the /k/ sound spelt ch (Greek in origin)		scheme, chorus, chemist, echo, character
Words with the /ʃ/ sound spelt ch (mostly French in origin)		chef, chalet, machine, brochure
Words ending with the /g/ sound spelt -gue and the /k/ sound spelt -que (French in origin)		league, tongue, antique, unique

Words with the /s/ sound spelt sc (Latin in origin)	In the Latin words from which these words come, the Romans probably pronounced the c and the k as two sounds rather than one – /s/ /k/.	science, scene, discipline, fascinate, crescent
Words with the /eɪ/ sound spelt ei, eigh, or ey		vein, weigh, eight, neighbour, they, obey
Possessive apostrophe with plural words	The apostrophe is placed after the plural form of the word; -s is not added if the plural already ends in -s, but is added if the plural does not end in -s (ie is an irregular plural – eg children's).	girls', boys', babies', children's, men's, mice's (Note: singular proper nouns ending in an s use the 's suffix eg Cyprus's population)
Homophones or near-homophones		accept/except, affect/effect, ball/bawl, berry/bury, brake/break, fair/fare, grate/great, groan/grown, here/hear, heel/heal/he'll, knot/not, mail/male, main/mane, meat/meet, medal/meddle, missed/mist, peace/piece, plain/plane, rain/rein/reign, scene/seen, weather/whether, whose/who's

Word list for Years 3 and 4

accident(ally)
actual(ly)
address
answer
appear
arrive
believe
bicycle
breath
breathe
build

busy/business
calendar
caught
centre
century
certain
circle
complete
consider
continue
decide

describe
different
difficult
disappear
early
earth
eight/eighth
enough
exercise
experience
experiment

extreme
famous
favourite
February
forward(s)
fruit
grammar
group
guard
guide
heard

heart
height
history
imagine
important
increase
interest
island
knowledge
learn
length

library
material
medicine
mention
minute
natural
naughty
notice
occasion(ally)
often
opposite

ordinary
particular
peculiar
perhaps
popular
position
possess(ion)
possible
potatoes
pressure
probably

promise
purpose
quarter
question
regular
reign
remember
sentence
separate
special
straight

strange
strength
suppose
therefore
though/although
thought
through
various
weight
woman/women

Teachers should continue to emphasise to pupils the relationships between sounds and letters, even when the relationships are unusual. Once root words are learned in this way, longer words can be spelled correctly, if the rules and guidelines for adding prefixes and suffixes are also known.

Examples:

business: once busy is learned, with due attention to the unusual spelling of the /i/ sound as 'u', business can then be spelled as **busy + ness**, with the **y** of **busy** changed to **i** according to the rule.

disappear: the root word **appear** contains sounds which can be spelled in more than one way so it needs to be learned, but the prefix **dis-** is then simply added to **appear**.

Understanding the relationships between words can also help with spelling.

Examples:

bicycle is *cycle* (from the Greek for wheel) with **bi-** (meaning *two*) before it.
medicine is related to *medical* so the /s/ sound is spelt as **c**.
opposite is related to *oppose*, so the schwa sound in *opposite* is spelt as **o**.

Years 5 and 6

Spelling - revise work done in previous years
Spelling - new work for Years 5 and 6

Statutory requirements	Rules and guidance (non-statutory)	Example words (non-statutory)
Endings which sound like /ʃəl/ **spelt -cious or -tious**	Not many common words end like this. If the root word ends in -**ce**, the /ʃ/ sound is usually spelt as **c** – eg vice – vicious, grace – gracious, space – spacious, malice – malicious. **Exception**: anxious.	vicious, precious, conscious, delicious, malicious, suspicious, ambitious, cautious, fictitious, infectious, nutritious
Endings which sound like /ʃl/	-**cial** is common after a vowel letter and -**tial** after a consonant letter, but there are some exceptions. **Exceptions**: initial, financial, commercial, provincial (the spelling of the last three is clearly related to finance, commerce and province).	official, special, artificial, partial, confidential, essential
Words ending in -ant, -ance/-ancy, -ent, -ence/-ency	Use -**ant** and -**ance/-ancy** if there is a related word with a /æ/ or /eɪ/ sound in the right position; -**ation** endings are often a clue. Use -**ent** and -**ence/-ency** after soft **c** (/s/ sound), soft **g** (/dʒ/ sound) and **qu**, or if there is a related word with a clear /ʃ/ sound in the right position. There are many words, however, where the above guidelines don't help. These words just have to be learned.	observant, observance, (observation), expectant (expectation), hesitant, hesitancy (hesitation), tolerant, tolerance (toleration), substance (substantial) innocent, innocence, decent, decency, frequent, frequency, confident, confidence (confidential) assistant, assistance, obedient, obedience, independent, independence
Words ending in -able and -ible **Words ending in -ably and -ibly**	The -**able/-ably** endings are far more common than the -**ible/-ibly** endings. As with -**ant** and -**ance/-ancy**, the -**able** ending is used if there is a related word ending in -**ation**. If the -**able** ending is added to a word ending in -**ce** or -**ge**, the **e** after the **c** or **g** must be kept as those letters would otherwise have their 'hard' sounds (as in cap and gap) before the **a** of the -**able** ending. The -**able** ending is usually but not always used if a complete root word can be heard before it, even if there is no related word ending in -**ation**. The first five examples opposite are obvious; in reliable, the complete word rely is heard, but the **y** changes to i in accordance with the rule. The -**ible** ending is common if a complete root word can't be heard before it but it also sometimes occurs when a complete word can be heard (eg sensible).	adorable/adorably (adoration), applicable/applicably (application), considerable/considerably (consideration), tolerable/tolerably (toleration) changeable, noticeable, forcible, legible dependable, comfortable, understandable, reasonable, enjoyable, reliable possible/possibly, horrible/horribly, terrible/terribly, visible/visibly, incredible/incredibly, sensible/sensibly

Topic	Rule	Examples
Adding suffixes beginning with vowel letters to words ending in -fer	The **r** is doubled if the **-fer** is still stressed when the ending is added. The **r** is not doubled if the **-fer** is no longer stressed.	referring, referred, referral, preferring, preferred, transferring, transferred, referee, referee, preference, transference
Use of the hyphen	Hyphens can be used to join a prefix to a root word, especially if the prefix ends in a vowel letter and the root word also begins with one.	co-ordinate, re-enter, co-operate, co-own
Words with the /iː/ sound spelt ei after c	The 'i before **e** except after **c**' rule applies to words where the sound spelt by **ei** is /iː/. **Exceptions:** *protein, caffeine, seize* (and *either* and *neither* if pronounced with an initial /iː/ sound).	deceive, conceive, receive, perceive, ceiling
Words containing the letter-string ough	**ough** is one of the trickiest spellings in English – it can be used to spell a number of different sounds.	ought, bought, thought, nought, brought, fought, rough, tough, enough, cough, though, although, dough, through, thorough, borough, plough, bough
Words with 'silent' letters (ie letters whose presence cannot be predicted from the pronunciation of the word)	Some letters which are no longer sounded used to be sounded hundreds of years ago: eg in *knight*, there was a /k/ sound before the /n/, and the **gh** used to represent the sound that 'ch' now represents in the Scottish word *loch*.	doubt, island, lamb, solemn, thistle, knight
Homophones and other words that are often confused	In these pairs of words, nouns end **-ce** and verbs end **-se**. Advice and advise provide a useful clue as the word *advise* (verb) is pronounced with a /z/ sound – which could not be spelt **c**. More examples: aisle: a gangway between seats (in a church, train, plane) isle: an island aloud: out loud allowed: permitted affect: usually a verb (eg *The weather may affect our plans*) effect: usually a noun (eg *It may have an effect on our plans*). If a verb, it means 'bring about' (eg *He will effect changes in the running of the business.*). altar: a table-like piece of furniture in a church alter: to change	advice/advise device/devise licence/license practice/practise prophecy/prophesy farther: further father: a male parent guessed: past tense of the verb *guess* guest: visitor heard: past tense of the verb *hear* herd: a group of animals led: past tense of the verb *lead* lead: present tense of that verb, or else the metal which is very heavy (*as heavy as lead*)

ascent: the act of ascending (going up)
assent: to agree/agreement (verb and noun)

bridal: to do with a bride at a wedding
bridle: reins etc for controlling a horse

cereal: made from grain (eg breakfast cereal)
serial: adjective from the noun *series* – a succession of things one after the other

compliment: to make nice remarks about someone (verb) or the remark that is made (noun)
complement: related to the word *complete* – to make something complete or more complete (eg *her scarf complemented her outfit*)

descent: the act of descending (going down)
dissent: to disagree/disagreement (verb and noun)

desert: as a noun – a barren place (stress on first syllable); as a verb – to abandon (stress on second syllable)
dessert: (stress on second syllable) a sweet course after the main course of a meal

draft: noun – a first attempt at writing something; verb – to make the first attempt; also, to draw in someone (eg *to draft in extra help*)
draught: a current of air

morning: before noon
mourning: grieving for someone who has died

past: noun or adjective referring to a previous time (eg *In the past*) or preposition or adverb showing place (eg *he walked past me*)
passed: past tense of the verb 'pass' (eg *I passed him in the road*)

precede: go in front of or before
proceed: go on

principal: adjective – most important (eg *principal ballerina*) noun – important person (eg *principal of a college*)
principle: basic truth or belief

profit: money that is made in selling things
prophet: someone who foretells the future

stationary: not moving
stationery: paper, envelopes etc

steal: take something that does not belong to you
steel: metal

wary: cautious
weary: tired

who's: contraction of *who is* or *who has*
whose: belonging to someone (eg *Whose jacket is that?*)

Word list for Years 5 and 6

accommodate
accompany
according
achieve
aggressive
amateur
ancient
apparent
appreciate
attached
available
average
awkward
bargain
bruise
category
cemetery
committee

communicate
community
competition
conscience*
conscious*
controversy
convenience
correspond
criticise (critic + ise)
curiosity
definite
desperate
determined
develop
dictionary
disastrous
embarrass

environment
equip (-ped, -ment)
especially
exaggerate
excellent
existence
explanation
familiar
foreign
forty
frequently
government
guarantee
harass
hindrance
identity
immediate(ly)

individual
interfere
interrupt
language
leisure
lightning
marvellous
mischievous
muscle
necessary
neighbour
nuisance
occupy
occur
opportunity
parliament
persuade
physical

prejudice
privilege
profession
programme
pronunciation
queue
recognise
recommend
relevant
restaurant
rhyme
rhythm
sacrifice
secretary
shoulder
signature
sincere(ly)
soldier

stomach
sufficient
suggest
symbol
system
temperature
thorough
twelfth
variety
vegetable
vehicle
yacht

Teachers should continue to emphasis to pupils the relationships between sounds and letters, even when the relationships are unusual. Once root words are learned in this way, longer words can be spelled correctly if the rules and guidelines for adding prefixes and suffixes are also known. Many of the words in the list above can be used for practice in adding suffixes.

Understanding the history of words and relationships between them can also help with spelling.

Examples:

* *Conscience* and *conscious* are related to *science*: *conscience* is simply *science* with the prefix *con-* added. These words come from the Latin word *scio* meaning *I know*.

The word *desperate*, meaning 'without hope', is often pronounced in English as *desp'rate*, but the *-sper-* part comes from the Latin *spero*, meaning 'I hope', in which the **e** was clearly sounded.

Familiar is related to *family*, so the /ə/ sound in the first syllable of *familiar* is spelt as **a**.

International Phonetic Alphabet

The table below shows each symbol of the International Phonetic Alphabet (IPA) and provides examples of the associated grapheme(s). [5]

The table is not a comprehensive alphabetic code chart; it is intended simply as guidance for teachers in understanding the IPA symbols used in the spelling appendix (English Appendix 1). The pronunciations in the table are, by convention, based on Received Pronunciation and could be significantly different from other accents.

Consonants

/b/	bad
/d/	dog
/ð/	this
/dʒ/	gem, jug
/f/	if, puff, photo
/g/	gum
/h/	how
/j/	yes
/k/	cat, check, key, school
/l/	leg, hill
/m/	man
/n/	man
/ŋ/	sing
/θ/	both
/p/	pet
/r/	red
/s/	sit, miss, cell
/ʃ/	she, chef
/t/	tea
/tʃ/	check
/v/	vet
/w/	wet, when
/z/	zip, hens, buzz
/ʒ/	pleasure

Vowels

/ɑː/	father, arm
/ɒ/	hot
/æ/	cat
/aɪ/	mind, fine, pie, high
/aʊ/	out, cow
/ɛ/	hen, head
/eɪ/	say, came, bait
/ɛə/	air
/əʊ/	cold, boat, cone, blow
/ɪ/	hit
/ɪə/	beer
/iː/	she, bead, see, scheme, chief
/ɔː/	launch, raw, born
/ɔɪ/	coin, boy
/ʊ/	book
/ʊə/	tour
/uː/	room, you, blue, brute
/ʌ/	cup
/ɜː/	fern, turn, girl
/ə/	farmer

[5] This chart is adapted slightly from the version provided on the DfE's website to support the Year 1 phonics screening check.

English Appendix 2: Vocabulary, grammar and punctuation

The grammar of our first language is learned naturally and implicitly through interactions with other speakers and from reading. Explicit knowledge of grammar is, however, very important, as it gives us more conscious control and choice in our language. Building this knowledge is best achieved through a focus on grammar within the teaching of reading, writing and speaking. Once pupils are familiar with a grammatical concept (for example 'modal verb'), they should be encouraged to apply and explore this concept in the grammar of their own speech and writing and to note where it is used by others. Young pupils, in particular, use more complex language in speech than in writing, and teachers should build on this, aiming for a smooth transition to sophisticated writing.

The table opposite focuses on Standard English and should be read in conjunction with the Programme of Study as it sets out the statutory requirements. The first column refers to the structure of words and vocabulary building. The table shows when concepts should be introduced first, not necessarily when they should be completely understood. It is very important, therefore, that the content in earlier years be revisited in subsequent years to consolidate knowledge and build on pupils' understanding. Teachers should also go beyond the content set out here if they feel it is appropriate.

The grammatical terms that pupils should learn are set out in the final column. They should learn to recognise and use the terminology through discussion and practice. All terms in bold should be understood with the meanings set out in the glossary.

Years 1 to 6 Detail of content to be introduced (statutory requirements)

Year	Word	Sentence	Text	Punctuation	Terminology for pupils
1	Regular **plural noun suffixes** -s or -es (for example, *dog, dogs; wish, wishes*), including the effects of these suffixes on the meaning of the noun. **Suffixes** that can be added to **verbs** where no change is needed in the spelling of root words (eg *helping, helped, helper*). How the **prefix** *un–* changes the meaning of **verbs** and **adjectives** (negation, *eg unkind*, or undoing, *eg untie the boat*).	How **words** can combine to make **sentences.** Joining **words** and joining **clauses** using *and.*	Sequencing **sentences** to form short narratives.	Separation of **words** with spaces. Introduction to capital letters, full stops, question marks and exclamation marks to demarcate **sentences.** Capital letters for names and for the personal **pronoun** *I.*	letter, capital letter word, singular, plural sentence punctuation, full stop, question mark, exclamation mark
2	Formation of **nouns** using **suffixes** such as *-ness, -er* and by compounding *(eg whiteboard, superman).* Formation of **adjectives** using **suffixes** such as -ful, -less. (A fuller list of **suffixes** can be found on page 45 in the Year 2 spelling section in English Appendix 1.) Use of the **suffixes** *-er, – est* in **adjectives** and -ly to turn adjectives into **adverbs.**	**Subordination** (using *when, if, that, because*) and coordination (using *or, and, but).* Expanded **noun phrases** for description and specification *(for example, the blue butterfly, plain flour, the man in the The Moon).* How the grammatical patterns in a sentence indicate its function as a **statement, question, exclamation** or **command.**	Correct choice and consistent use of **present tense** and **past tense** throughout writing. Use of the **progressive** form of **verbs** in the **present** and **past tense** to mark actions in progress *(for example, she is drumming, he was shouting).*	Use of capital letters, full stops, question marks and exclamation marks to demarcate **sentences.** Commas to separate items in a list. **Apostrophes** to mark where letters are missing in spelling and to mark singular possession in nouns (for example, the girl's name).	noun, noun phrase statement, question, exclamation, command, compound, adjective, verb, suffix adverb tense (past, present) apostrophe, comma

	Word	Sentence	Text	Punctuation	Terminology for pupils
3	Formation of **nouns** using a range of **prefixes**, for example, *super-, anti-, auto-*. Use of the **forms** *a* or *an* according to whether the next **word** begins with a **consonant** or a **vowel** (for example, *a rock, an open box*). **Word families** based on common **words**, showing how words are related in form and meaning (for example, *solve, solution, solver, dissolve, insoluble*).	Expressing time, place and cause using **conjunctions** (for example, *when, before, after, while, so, because*), **adverbs** (for example, *then, next, soon, therefore*), or **prepositions** (for example, *before, after, during, in, because of*).	Introduction to paragraphs as a way to group related material. Headings and subheadings to aid presentation. Use of the **present perfect** form of **verbs** instead of the simple past (for example, *He has gone out to play* contrasted with *He went out to play*).	Introduction to inverted commas to **punctuate** direct speech.	adverb, preposition conjunction word family, prefix clause, subordinate clause direct speech consonant, consonant letter, vowel, vowel letter inverted commas (or 'speech marks')
4	The grammatical difference between **plural** and **possessive** -s. Standard English forms for **verb inflections** instead of local spoken forms (for example, *we were* instead of *we was*, or *I did* instead of *I done*).	Noun phrases expanded by the addition of modifying adjectives, nouns and preposition phrases (eg *the teacher* expanded to: *the strict maths teacher with curly hair*). **Fronted adverbials** (for example, *Later that day, I heard the bad news.*).	Use of paragraphs to organise ideas around a theme. Appropriate choice of **pronoun** or **noun** within and across **sentences** to aid cohesion and avoid repetition.	Use of inverted commas and other **punctuation** to indicate direct speech, for example, a comma after the reporting clause; end punctuation within inverted commas: *The conductor shouted, 'Sit down!'*). **Apostrophes** to mark singular and **plural** possession (for example, *the girl's name, the girls' names*) Use of commas after **fronted adverbials**.	determiner pronoun, possessive pronoun, adverbial

5	Converting **nouns** or **adjectives** into **verbs** using **suffixes** (for example, -ate; -ise; -ify). **Verb prefixes** (for example, dis-, de-, mis-, over- and re-).	**Relative clauses** beginning with *who, which, where, when, whose, that,* or an omitted relative pronoun. Indicating degrees of possibility using **adverbs** (for example, *perhaps, surely*) or **modal verbs** (for example, *might, should, will, must*).	Devices to build **cohesion** within a paragraph (for example, *then, after that, this, firstly*). Linking ideas across paragraphs using **adverbials** of time (for example, *later*), place (for example, *nearby*) and number (for example, *secondly*) or tense choices (for example, he *had seen her before*)	Brackets, dashes or commas to indicate parenthesis. Use of commas to clarify meaning or avoid ambiguity.	modal verb, relative pronoun relative clause parenthesis, bracket, dash cohesion, ambiguity
6	The difference between vocabulary typical of informal speech and vocabulary appropriate for formal speech and writing (for example, *find out – discover; ask for – request; go in – enter*). How words are related by meaning as synonyms and antonyms (eg *big, large, little*).	Use of the **passive** to affect the presentation of information in a **sentence** (for example, *I broke the window in the greenhouse* versus *The window in the greenhouse was broken [by me]*). The difference between structures typical of informal speech and structures appropriate for formal speech and writing (for example, the use of question tags: *He's your friend, isn't he?*, or the use of **subjunctive** forms such as *If I were* or *Were they to come* in some very formal writing and speech).	Linking ideas across paragraphs using a wider range of **cohesive devices**: repetition of a **word** or phrase, grammatical connections (for example, *the use of adverbials such as on the other hand, in contrast, or as a consequence*), and **ellipsis**. Layout devices, for example, headings, subheadings, columns, bullets, or tables, to structure text.	Use of the semi-colon, colon and dash to mark the boundary between independent **clauses** (for example, *It's raining; I'm fed up*). Use of the colon to introduce a list and use of semi-colons within lists. **Punctuation** of bullet points to list information. How hyphens can be used to avoid ambiguity (for example, *man eating shark* versus *man-eating shark*, or *recover* versus *re-cover*).	subject, object active, passive synonym, antonym ellipsis, hyphen, colon, semi-colon, bullet points

Glossary for the Programmes of Study for English (non-statutory)

The following glossary includes all the technical grammatical terms used in the Programmes of Study for English, as well as others that might be useful. It is intended as an aid for teachers, not as the body of knowledge that should be learned by pupils. Apart from a few which are used only in schools (eg *root word*), the terms below are used with the meanings defined here in most modern books on English grammar. It is recognised that there are different schools of thought on grammar, but the terms defined here clarify those being used in the Programmes of Study. For further details, teachers should consult the many books that are available.

Terms in definitions

As in any tightly structured area of knowledge, grammar, vocabulary and spelling involve a network of technical concepts that help to define each other. Consequently, the definition of one concept builds on other concepts that are equally technical. Concepts that are defined elsewhere in the glossary are hyperlinked. For some concepts, the technical definition may be slightly different from the meaning that some teachers may have learned at school or may have been using with their own pupils; in these cases, the more familiar meaning is also discussed.

active voice	An active verb has its usual pattern of subject and object (in contrast with the passive).	Active: The school arranged a visit. Passive: A visit was arranged by the school.
adjective	The surest way to identify adjectives is by the ways they can be used: • before a noun, to make the noun's meaning more specific (ie to modify the noun), or • after the verb be, as its complement. Adjectives cannot be modified by other adjectives. This distinguishes them from nouns, which can be. Adjectives are sometimes called 'describing words' because they pick out single characteristics such as size or colour. This is often true, but it doesn't help to distinguish adjectives from other word classes, because verbs, nouns and adverbs can do the same thing.	The pupils did some really good work. [adjective used before a noun, to modify it] Their work was good. [adjective used after the verb be, as its complement] Not adjectives: The lamp glowed. [verb] It was such a bright red! [noun] He spoke loudly. [adverb] It was a French grammar book. [noun]
adverb	The surest way to identify adverbs is by the ways they can be used: they can modify a verb, an adjective, another adverb or even a whole clause. Adverbs are sometimes said to describe manner or time. This is often true, but it doesn't help to distinguish adverbs from other word classes that can be used as adverbials, such as preposition phrases, noun phrases and subordinate clauses.	Usha soon started snoring loudly. [adverbs modifying the verbs started and snoring] That match was really exciting! [adverb modifying the adjective exciting] We don't get to play games very often. [adverb modifying the other adverb, often] Fortunately, it didn't rain. [adverb modifying the whole clause 'it didn't rain' by commenting on it] Not adverbs: Usha went up the stairs. [preposition phrase used as adverbial] She finished her work this evening. [noun phrase used as adverbial] She finished when the teacher got cross. [subordinate clause used as adverbial]
adverbial	An adverbial is a word or phrase that is used, like an adverb, to modify a verb or clause. Of course, adverbs can be used as adverbials, but many other types of words and phrases can be used this way, including preposition phrases and subordinate clauses.	The bus leaves in five minutes. [preposition phrase as adverbial: modifies leaves] She promised to see him last night. [noun phrase modifying either promised or see, according to the intended meaning] She worked until she had finished. [subordinate clause as adverbial]
antonym	Two words are antonyms if their meanings are opposites.	hot – cold light – dark light – heavy
apostrophe	Apostrophes have two completely different uses: • showing the place of missing letters (eg I'm for I am) • marking possessives (eg Hannah's mother).	I'm going out and I won't be long. [showing missing letters] Hannah's mother went to town in Justin's car. [marking possessives]
article	The articles the (definite) and a or an (indefinite) are the most common type of determiner.	The dog found a bone in an old box.

Term	Description	Example(s)
auxiliary verb	The auxiliary verbs are *be, have* and *do* and the modal verbs. They can be used to make questions and negative statements. In addition: • *be* is used in the progressive and passive • *have* is used in the perfect • *do* is used to form questions and negative statements if no other auxiliary verb is present	They <u>are</u> winning the match. [be used in the progressive] Have you finished your picture? [have used to make a question, and the perfect] No, I <u>don't</u> know him. [do used to make a negative; no other auxiliary is present] Will you come with me or not? [modal verb will used to make a question about the other person's willingness]
clause	A clause is a special type of phrase whose head is a verb. Clauses can sometimes be complete sentences. Clauses may be main or subordinate. Traditionally, a clause had to have a finite verb, but most modern grammarians also recognise non-finite clauses.	It was raining. [single-clause sentence] It was raining but <u>we were indoors</u>. [two finite clauses] If you are coming to the party, please let us know. [finite subordinate clause inside a finite main clause] Usha went upstairs <u>to play on her computer</u>. [non-finite clause]
cohesion	A text has cohesion if it is clear how the meanings of its parts fit together. Cohesive devices can help to do this. In the example, there are repeated references to the same thing (shown by the **bold text** and underlines), and the logical relations, such as time and cause, between different parts are clear.	**A visit** has been arranged for Year 6, to the *Mountain Peaks Field Study Centre, leaving school at 9.30am.* **This is *an overnight visit*.** *The centre* has beautiful grounds and a ***nature trail****. During the afternoon, the children will follow* **the trail***.
cohesive device	Cohesive devices are words used to show how the different parts of a text fit together. In other words, they create cohesion. Some examples of cohesive devices are: • determiners and pronouns, which can refer back to earlier words • conjunctions and adverbs, which can make relations between words clear • ellipsis of expected words.	Julia's dad bought her a football. <u>The football</u> was expensive! <u>The football was expensive!</u> [determiner; refers us back to a particular football] Joe was given a bike for Christmas. He liked <u>it</u> very much. [the pronouns refer back to Joe and the bike] We'll be going shopping <u>before</u> we go to the park. [conjunction; makes a relationship of time clear] I'm afraid we're going to have to wait for the next train. <u>Meanwhile</u>, we could have a cup of tea. [adverb; refers back to the time of waiting] Where are you going? [...] To school! [ellipsis of the expected words I'm going; links the answer back to the question]
complement	A verb's subject complement adds more information about its subject, and its object complement does the same for its object. Unlike the verb's object, its complement may be an adjective. The verb *be* normally has a complement.	She is <u>our teacher</u>. [adds more information about the subject, she] They seem <u>very competent</u>. [adds more information about the subject, they] Learning makes me <u>happy</u>. [adds more information about the object, me]
compound, compounding	A compound word contains at least two root words in its morphology; eg *whiteboard, superman.* Compounding is very important in English.	*blackbird, blow-dry, bookshop, ice-cream, English teacher, inkjet, one-eyed, bone-dry, baby-sit, daydream, outgrow*

SCHOLASTIC

Term	Definition	Example
conjunction	A conjunction links two words or phrases together. There are two main types of conjunctions: • co-ordinating conjunctions (eg *and*) link two words or phrases together as an equal pair • subordinating conjunctions (eg *when*) introduce a subordinate clause.	*James bought a bat and ball.* [links the words *bat* and *ball* as an equal pair] *Kylie is young but she can kick the ball hard.* [links two clauses as an equal pair] *Everyone watches when Kyle does back-flips.* [introduces a subordinate clause] *Joe can't practise kicking because he's injured.* [introduces a subordinate clause]
consonant	A sound which is produced when the speaker closes off or obstructs the flow of air through the vocal tract, usually using lips, tongue or teeth. Most of the letters of the alphabet represent consonants. Only the letters *a, e, i, o, u* and *y* can represent vowel sounds.	/p/ [flow of air stopped by the lips, then released] /t/ [flow of air stopped by the tongue touching the roof of the mouth, then released] /f/ [flow of air obstructed by the bottom lip touching the top teeth] /s/ [flow of air obstructed by the tip of the tongue touching the gum line]
continuous	See progressive	
co-ordinate, co-ordination	Words or phrases are coordinated if they are linked as an equal pair by a coordinating conjunction (ie *and, but, or*). In the examples on the right, the co-ordinated elements are shown in the same colour, and the conjunction is underlined. The difference between coordination and subordination is that, in subordination, the two linked elements are not equal.	*Susan and Amra met in a café.* [links the words *Susan* and *Amra* as an equal pair] *They talked and drank tea for an hour.* [links two clauses as an equal pair] *Susan got a bus but Amra walked.* [links two clauses as an equal pair] Not coordination: *They ate before they met.* [*before* introduces a subordinate clause]
determiner	A determiner specifies a noun as known or unknown, and it goes before any modifiers (eg adjectives or other nouns). Some examples of determiners are: • articles (*the, a* or *an*) • demonstratives (eg *this, those*) • possessives (eg *my, your*) • quantifiers (eg *some, every*).	the home team [article, specifies the team as known] a good team [article, specifies the team as unknown] that child [demonstrative, known] Julia's parents [possessive, known] some big boys [quantifier, unknown] Contrast: home the team; big some boys [both incorrect, because the determiner should come before other modifiers]
digraph	A type of grapheme where two letters represent one phoneme. Sometimes, these two letters are not next to one another; this is called a split digraph.	The digraph ea in *each* is pronounced /i:/. The digraph sh in *shed* is pronounced /ʃ/. The split digraph i–e in *line* is pronounced /aɪ/.
ellipsis	Ellipsis is the omission of a word or phrase which is expected and predictable.	*Frankie waved to Ivana and she watched her drive away.* *She did it because she wanted to do it.*

Term	Definition	Example
etymology	A word's etymology is its history: its origins in earlier forms of English or other languages, and how its form and meaning have changed. Many words in English have come from Greek, Latin or French.	The word *school* was borrowed from a Greek word ό-ïẽþ (*skholé*) meaning 'leisure'. The word *verb* comes from Latin *verbum*, meaning 'word'. The word *mutton* comes from French *mouton*, meaning 'sheep'.
finite verb	Every sentence typically has at least one verb which is either past or present tense. Such verbs are called 'finite'. The imperative verb in a command is also finite. Verbs that are not finite, such as participles or infinitives, cannot stand on their own: they are linked to another verb in the sentence.	Lizzie *does* the dishes every day. [present tense] Even Hana *did* the dishes yesterday. [past tense] *Do* the dishes, Naser! [imperative] Not finite verbs: I have *done* them. [combined with the finite verb *have*] I will *do* them. [combined with the finite verb *will*] I want to *do* them! [combined with the finite verb *want*]
fronting, fronted	A word or phrase that normally comes after the verb may be moved before the verb: when this happens, we say it has been 'fronted'. For example, a fronted adverbial is an adverbial which has been moved before the verb. When writing fronted phrases, we often follow them with a comma.	*Before we begin*, make sure you've got a pencil. [Without fronting: Make sure you've got a pencil before we begin.] *The day after tomorrow*, I'm visiting my granddad. [Without fronting: I'm visiting my granddad the day after tomorrow.]
future	Reference to future time can be marked in a number of different ways in English. All these ways involve the use of a present-tense verb. See also tense. Unlike many other languages (such as French, Spanish or Italian), English has no distinct 'future tense' form of the verb comparable with its present and past tenses.	He *will* leave tomorrow. [present-tense *will* followed by infinitive *leave*] He *may* leave tomorrow. [present-tense *may* followed by infinitive *leave*] He *leaves* tomorrow. [present-tense *leaves*] He *is going to leave* tomorrow. [present tense *is* followed by *going to* plus the infinitive *leave*]
GPC	See grapheme-phoneme correspondences.	
grapheme	A letter, or combination of letters, that corresponds to a single phoneme within a word.	The grapheme *t* in the words *ten*, *bet* and *ate* corresponds to the phoneme /t/. The grapheme *ph* in the word *dolphin* corresponds to the phoneme /f/.
grapheme-phoneme correspondences	The links between letters, or combinations of letters, (graphemes) and the speech sounds (phonemes) that they represent. In the English writing system, graphemes may correspond to different phonemes in different words.	The grapheme *s* corresponds to the phoneme /s/ in the word *see*, but... ...it corresponds to the phoneme /z/ in the word *easy*.
head	See phrase	
homonym	Two different words are homonyms if they both look exactly the same when written, and sound exactly the same when pronounced.	Has he *left* yet? Yes – he went through the door on the *left*. Trees have *bark*. The noise a dog makes is called a *bark*.

homophone	Two different words are homophones if they sound exactly the same when pronounced.	*hear, here* *some, sum*
infinitive	A verb's infinitive is the basic form used as the head-word in a dictionary (eg walk, be). Infinitives are often used: • after *to* • after <u>modal verbs</u>.	*I want to <u>walk</u>.* *I will be quiet.*
inflection	When we add *-ed* to *walk*, or change *mouse* to *mice*, this change of <u>morphology</u> produces an inflection ('bending') of the basic word which has special grammar (eg <u>past tense or plural</u>). In contrast, adding *-er* to *walk* produces a completely different word, *walker*, which is part of the same <u>word family</u>. Inflection is sometimes thought of as merely a change of ending, but, in fact, some words change completely when inflected.	*dogs* is an inflection of *dog*. *went* is an inflection of *go*. *better* is an inflection of *good*.
intransitive verb	A verb which does not need an object in a sentence to complete its meaning. See 'transitive verb'.	*The old woman <u>died</u>.* *We all <u>laughed</u>.*
main clause	A <u>sentence</u> contains at least one <u>clause</u> which is not a <u>subordinate clause</u>; such a clause is a main clause. A main clause may contain any number of subordinate clauses.	*<u>It was raining</u> but <u>the sun was shining</u>.* [Two main clauses] *<u>The man who wrote it told me that it was true</u>.* [One main clause containing two subordinate clauses.] *She said, '<u>It rained all day.</u>'* [One main clause containing another.]
modal verb	Modal verbs are used to change the meaning of other <u>verbs</u>. They can express meanings such as certainty, ability, or obligation. The main modal verbs are *will, would, can, could, may, might, shall, should, must* and *ought*. A modal verb only has <u>finite</u> forms and has no <u>suffixes</u> (eg *I sing – he sings*, but not *I must – he musts*).	*I <u>can</u> do this maths work by myself.* *This ride <u>may</u> be too scary for you!* *You <u>should</u> help your little brother.* *Is it going to rain? Yes, it <u>might</u>.* *Canning swim is important.* [not possible because *can* must be finite; contrast: *Being able to swim is important*, where *being* is not a modal verb]
modify, modifier	One word or phrase modifies another by making its meaning more specific. Because the two words make a <u>phrase</u>, the 'modifier' is normally close to the modified word.	In the phrase *primary-school teacher, teacher* is modified by *primary-school* (to mean a specific kind of teacher) *school* is modified by *primary* (to mean a specific kind of school).

Term	Definition	Examples
morphology	A word's morphology is its internal make-up in terms of root words and suffixes or prefixes, as well as other kinds of change such as the change of mouse to mice. Morphology may be used to produce different inflections of the same word (eg boy – boys), or entirely new words (eg boy – boyish) belonging to the same word family. A word that contains two or more root words is a compound (eg news+paper, ice+cream).	dogs has the morphological make-up: dog + s. unhelpfulness has the morphological make-up: unhelpful + ness where unhelpful = un + helpful and helpful = help + ful
noun	The surest way to identify nouns is by the ways they can be used after determiners such as the: for example, most nouns will fit into the frame 'The ... matters/matter.' Nouns are sometimes called 'naming words' because they name people, places and 'things'; this is often true, but it doesn't help to distinguish nouns from other word classes. For example, prepositions can name places and verbs can name 'things' such as actions. Nouns may be classified as **common** (eg boy, day) or proper (eg Ivan, Wednesday), and also as **countable** (eg thing, boy) or non-countable (eg stuff, money). These classes can be recognised by the determiners they combine with.	Our dog bit the burglar on his behind! My big brother did an amazing jump on his skateboard. Actions speak louder than words. Not nouns: He's behind you! [this names a place, but is a preposition, not a noun] She can jump so high! [this names an action, but is a verb, not a noun] common, countable: a book, books, two chocolates, one day, fewer ideas common, non-countable: money, some chocolate, less imagination proper, countable: Marilyn, London, Wednesday
noun phrase	A noun phrase is a phrase with a noun as its head, eg some foxes, foxes with bushy tails. Some grammarians recognise one-word phrases, so that foxes are multiplying would contain the noun foxes acting as the head of the noun phrase foxes.	Adult foxes can jump. [adult modifies foxes, so adult belongs to the noun phrase] Almost all healthy adult foxes in this area can jump. [all the other words help to modify foxes, so they all belong to the noun phrase]
object	An object is normally a noun, pronoun or noun phrase that comes straight after the verb, and shows what the verb is acting upon. Objects can be turned into the subject of a passive verb, and cannot be adjectives (contrast with complements).	Year 2 designed puppets. [noun acting as object] I like that. [pronoun acting as object] Some people suggested a pretty display. [noun phrase acting as object] Contrast: A display was suggested. [object of active verb becomes the subject of the passive verb] Year 2 designed pretty. [incorrect, because adjectives cannot be objects]

Term	Description	Examples
participle	Verbs in English have two participles, called 'present participle' (eg *walking, taking*) and 'past participle' (eg *walked, taken*). Unfortunately, these terms can be confusing to learners, because: • they don't necessarily have anything to do with present or past time • although past participles are used as perfects (eg *has eaten*) they are also used as passives (eg *was eaten*).	*He is walking to school.* [present participle in a progressive] *He has taken the bus to school.* [past participle in a perfect] *The photo was taken in the rain.* [past participle in a passive]
passive	The sentence *It was eaten by our dog* is the passive of *Our dog ate it.* A passive is recognisable from: • the past participle form *eaten* • the normal object (*it*) turned into the subject • the normal subject (*our dog*) turned into an optional preposition phrase with *by* as its head • the verb *be* (*was*), or some other verb such as *get.* Contrast active. A verb is not 'passive' just because it has a passive meaning: it must be the passive version of an active verb.	*A visit was arranged by the school.* *Our cat got run over by a bus.* Active versions: *The school arranged a visit.* *A bus ran over our cat.* Not passive: *He received a warning.* [past tense, active *received*] *We had an accident.* [past tense, active *had*]
past tense	Verbs in the past tense are commonly used to: • talk about the past • talk about imagined situations • make a request sound more polite. Most verbs take a suffix -*ed*, to form their past tense, but many commonly-used verbs are irregular. See also tense.	*Tom and Chris showed me their new TV.* [names an event in the past] *Antonio went on holiday to Brazil.* [names an event in the past; irregular past of *go*] *I wish I had a puppy.* [names an imagined situation, not a situation in the past] *I was hoping you'd help tomorrow.* [makes an implied request sound more polite]
perfect	The perfect form of a verb generally calls attention to the consequences of a prior event; for example, *He has gone to lunch* implies that he is still away, in contrast with *He went to lunch.* It is formed by: • turning the verb into its past participle inflection • adding a form of the verb *have* before it. It can also be combined with the progressive (eg *he has been going*).	*She has downloaded some songs.* [present perfect; now she has some songs] *I had eaten lunch when you came.* [past perfect; I wasn't hungry when you came]

Term	Definition	Example
phoneme	A phoneme is the smallest unit of sound that signals a distinct, contrasting meaning. For example: • /t/ contrasts with /k/ to signal the difference between *tap* and *cap* • /t/ contrasts with /l/ to signal the difference between *bought* and *ball*. It is this contrast in meaning that tells us there are two distinct phonemes at work. There are around 44 phonemes in English; the exact number depends on regional accents. A single phoneme may be represented in writing by one, two, three or four letters constituting a single <u>grapheme</u>.	The word *cat* has three letters and three phonemes: /kæt/ The word *catch* has five letters and three phonemes: /katʃ/ The word *caught* has six letters and three phonemes: /kɔːt/
phrase	A phrase is a group of words that are grammatically connected so that they stay together, and that expand a single word, called the 'head'. The phrase is a <u>noun phrase</u> if its head is a noun, a <u>preposition phrase</u> if its head is a preposition, and so on; but if the head is a <u>verb</u>, the phrase is called a <u>clause</u>. Phrases can be made up of other phrases.	*She waved to <u>her mother</u>.* [A noun phrase, with the noun *mother* as its head] *She waved <u>to her mother</u>.* [A preposition phrase, with the preposition *to* as its head] *<u>She waved to her mother</u>.* [A clause, with the verb *waved* as its head]
plural	A plural <u>noun</u> normally has a <u>suffix</u> -s or -es and means 'more than one'. There are a few nouns with different <u>morphology</u> in the plural (eg *mice, formulae*).	<u>dogs</u> [more than one dog]; <u>boxes</u> [more than one box] <u>mice</u> [more than one mouse]
possessive	A possessive can be: • a <u>noun</u> followed by an <u>apostrophe</u>, with or without s • a possessive <u>pronoun</u>. The relation expressed by a possessive goes well beyond ordinary ideas of 'possession'. A possessive may act as a <u>determiner</u>.	<u>Tariq's</u> *book* [Tariq has the book] *The <u>boys'</u> arrival* [the boys arrive] <u>His</u> *obituary* [the obituary is about him] *That essay is <u>mine</u>.* [I wrote the essay]
prefix	A prefix is added at the beginning of a <u>word</u> in order to turn it into another word. Contrast <u>suffix</u>.	<u>over</u>take, <u>dis</u>appear
preposition	A preposition links a following <u>noun</u>, <u>pronoun</u> or <u>noun phrase</u> to some other word in the sentence. Prepositions often describe locations or directions, but can describe other things, such as relations of time. Words like *before* or *since* can act either as prepositions or as <u>conjunctions</u>.	*Tom waved goodbye <u>to</u> Christy. She'll be back <u>from</u> Australia <u>in</u> two weeks.* *I haven't seen my dog <u>since</u> this morning.* Contrast: *I'm going, <u>since</u> no-one wants me here!* [conjunction: links two clauses]

■SCHOLASTIC

preposition phrase	A preposition phrase has a preposition as its head followed by a noun, pronoun or noun phrase.	*He was <u>in bed</u>.* *I met them <u>after the party</u>.*
present tense	<u>Verbs</u> in the present tense are commonly used to: • talk about the <u>present</u> • talk about the <u>future</u>. They may take a suffix -s (depending on the <u>subject</u>). See also <u>tense</u>.	*Jamal <u>goes</u> to the pool every day.* [describes a habit that exists now] *He <u>can</u> swim.* [describes a state that is true now] *The bus <u>arrives</u> at three.* [scheduled now] *My friends <u>are</u> coming to play.* [describes a plan in progress now]
progressive	The progressive (also known as the 'continuous') form of a <u>verb</u> generally describes events in progress. It is formed by combining the verb's present <u>participle</u> (eg *singing*) with a form of the verb be (eg *he was singing*). The progressive can also be combined with the <u>perfect</u> (eg *he has been singing*).	*Michael <u>is singing</u> in the store room.* [present progressive] *Amanda <u>was making</u> a patchwork quilt.* [past progressive] *Usha <u>had been practising</u> for an hour when I called.* [past perfect progressive]
pronoun	Pronouns are normally used like <u>nouns</u>, except that: • they are grammatically more specialised • it is harder to <u>modify</u> them In the examples, each sentence is written twice: once with nouns, and once with pronouns (underlined). Where the same thing is being talked about, the words are shown in bold.	**Amanda** *waved to* **Michael**. <u>**She**</u> *waved to* <u>**him**</u>. **John's** *mother is over there.* <u>**His**</u> *mother is over there.* *The* **visit** *will be an overnight* **visit**. <u>**This**</u> *will be an overnight* **visit**. **Simon** *is the one:* **Simon** *broke it.* <u>**He**</u> *is the one* <u>**who**</u> *broke it.*
punctuation	Punctuation includes any conventional features of writing other than spelling and general layout: the standard punctuation marks . , ; : ? ! – – ( ) " " ' ' , and also word-spaces, capital letters, apostrophes, paragraph breaks and bullet points. One important role of punctuation is to indicate <u>sentence</u> boundaries.	*<u>"I'm going out, Usha, and I won't be long,"</u> <u>Mum said.</u>*
Received pronunciation	Received Pronunciation (often abbreviated to RP) is an accent which is used only by a small minority of English speakers in England. It is not associated with any one region. Because of its regional neutrality, it is the accent which is generally shown in dictionaries in the UK (but not, of course, in the USA). RP has no special status in the National Curriculum.	
register	Classroom lessons, football commentaries and novels use different registers of the same language, recognised by differences of vocabulary and grammar. Registers are 'varieties' of a language which are each tied to a range of uses, in contrast with dialects, which are tied to groups of users.	*I regret to inform you that Mr Joseph Smith has passed away.* [formal letter] *Have you heard that Joe has died?* [casual speech] *Joe falls down and dies, centre stage.* [stage direction]

Term	Definition	Examples
relative clause	A relative clause is a special type of subordinate clause that modifies a noun. It often does this by using a relative pronoun such as *who* or *that* to refer back to that noun, though the relative pronoun *that* is often omitted. A relative clause may also be attached to a clause. In that case, the pronoun refers back to the whole clause, rather than referring back to a noun. In the examples, the relative clauses are underlined, and the colour-coding pairs the pronouns with the words they refer back to.	That's the **boy who** lives near school. [*who* refers back to *boy*] The **prize that** I won was a book. [*that* refers back to *prize*] The **prize** I won was a book. [the pronoun *that* is omitted] **Tom broke the game, which** annoyed Ali. [*which* refers back to the whole clause]
root word	Morphology breaks words down into root words, which can stand alone, and suffixes or prefixes which can't. For example, *help* is the root word for other words in its word family such as *helpful* and *helpless*, and also for its inflections such as *helping*. Compound words (eg *help-desk*) contain two or more root words. When looking in a dictionary, we sometimes have to look for the root word (or words) of the word we are interested in.	*played* [the root word is *play*] *unfair* [the root word is *fair*] *football* [the root words are *foot* and *ball*]
schwa	The name of a vowel sound that is found only in unstressed positions in English. It is the most common vowel sound in English. It is written as /ə/ in the International Phonetic Alphabet. In the English writing system, it can be written in many different ways.	/əlɒŋ/ [*along*] /bʌtə/ [*butter*] /dɒktə/ [*doctor*]
sentence	A sentence is a group of words which are grammatically connected to each other but not to any words outside the sentence. The form of a sentence's main clause shows whether it is being used as a statement, a question, a command or an exclamation. A sentence may consist of a single clause or it may contain several clauses held together by subordination or coordination. Classifying sentences as 'simple', 'complex' or 'compound' can be confusing, because a 'simple' sentence may be complicated, and a 'complex' one may be straightforward. The terms '**single-clause sentence**' and '**multi-clause sentence**' may be more helpful.	*John went to his friend's house. He stayed there till tea-time.* *John went to his friend's house, he stayed there till tea-time.* [This is a 'comma splice', a common error in which a comma is used where either a full stop or a semi-colon is needed to indicate the lack of any grammatical connection between the two clauses]. *You are my friend.* [statement] *Are you my friend?* [question] *Be my friend!* ['command'] *What a good friend you are!* [exclamation] *Ali went home on his bike to his goldfish and his current library book about pets.* [single-clause sentence] *She went shopping but took back everything she had bought because she didn't like any of it.* [multi-clause sentence]

SCHOLASTIC

Term	Definition	Examples
split digraph	See digraph.	
Standard English	Standard English can be recognised by the use of a very small range of forms such as those books, I did it and I wasn't doing anything (rather than their non-Standard equivalents); it is not limited to any particular accent. It is the variety of English which is used, with only minor variation, as a major world language. Some people use Standard English all the time, in all situations from the most casual to the most formal, so it covers most registers. The aim of the National Curriculum is that everyone should be able to use Standard English as needed in writing and in relatively formal speaking.	I did it because they were not willing to undertake any more work on those houses. [formal Standard English] I did it cos they wouldn't do any more work on those houses. [casual Standard English] I done it cos they wouldn't do no more work on them houses. [casual non-Standard English]
stress	A syllable is stressed if it is pronounced more forcefully than the syllables next to it. The other syllables are unstressed.	about visit
subject	The subject of a verb is normally the noun, noun phrase or pronoun that names the 'do-er' or 'be-er'. The subject's normal position is: • just before the verb in a statement • just after the auxiliary verb, in a question. Unlike the verb's object and complement, the subject can determine the form of the verb (eg I am, you are).	Rula's mother went out. That is uncertain. The children will study the animals. Will the children study the animals?
subjunctive	In some languages, the inflections of a verb include a large range of special forms which are used typically in subordinate clauses, and are called 'subjunctives'. English has very few such forms and those it has tend to be used in rather formal styles.	The school requires that all pupils be honest. The school rules demand that pupils not enter the gym at lunchtime. If Zoë were the class president, things would be much better.
subordinate, subordination	A subordinate word or phrase tells us more about the meaning of the word it is subordinate to. Subordination can be thought of as an unequal relationship between a subordinate word and a main word. For example: • an adjective is subordinate to the noun it modifies • subjects and objects are subordinate to their verbs. Subordination is much more common than the equal relationship of coordination. See also subordinate clause.	big dogs [big is subordinate to dogs] Big dogs need long walks. [big dogs and long walks are subordinate to need] We can watch TV when we've finished. [when we've finished is subordinate to watch]

Term	Definition	Examples
subordinate clause	A clause which is subordinate to some other part of the same sentence is a subordinate clause; for example, in *The apple that I ate was sour*, the clause *that I ate* is subordinate to *apple* (which it modifies). Subordinate clauses contrast with coordinate clauses as in *It was sour but looked very tasty*. (Contrast: main clause) However, clauses that are directly quoted as direct speech are not subordinate clauses.	*That's the street where Ben lives.* [relative clause; modifies *street*] *He watched her as she disappeared.* [adverbial; modifies *watched*] *What you said was very nice.* [acts as subject of *was*] *She noticed an hour had passed.* [acts as object of *noticed*] Not subordinate: *He shouted, 'Look out!'*
suffix	A suffix is an 'ending', used at the end of one word to turn it into another word. Unlike root words, suffixes cannot stand on their own as a complete word. Contrast prefix.	*call – called* *teach – teacher* [turns a verb into a noun] *terror – terrorise* [turns a noun into a verb] *green – greenish* [leaves word class unchanged]
syllable	A syllable sounds like a beat in a word. Syllables consist of at least one vowel, and possibly one or more consonants.	*Cat* has one syllable. *Fairy* has two syllables. *Hippopotamus* has five syllables.
synonym	Two words are synonyms if they have the same meaning, or similar meanings. Contrast antonym.	*talk – speak* *old – elderly*
tense	In English, tense is the choice between present and past verbs, which is special because it is signalled by inflections and normally indicates differences of time. In contrast, languages like French, Spanish and Italian have three or more distinct tense forms, including a future tense. (See also: future.) The simple tenses (present and past) may be combined in English with the perfect and progressive.	*He studies.* [present tense – present time] *He studied yesterday.* [past tense – past time] *He studies tomorrow, or else!* [present tense – future time] *He may study tomorrow.* [present tense + infinitive – future time] *He plans to study tomorrow.* [present tense + infinitive – future time] *If he studied tomorrow, he'd see the difference.* [past tense – imagined future] Contrast three distinct tense forms in Spanish: *Estudia.* [present tense] *Estudió.* [past tense] *Estudiará.* [future tense]
transitive verb	A transitive verb takes at least one object in a sentence to complete its meaning, in contrast to an intransitive verb, which does not.	*He loves Juliet.* *She understands English grammar.*
trigraph	A type of grapheme where three letters represent one phoneme.	*High, pure, patch, hedge*
unstressed	See stressed.	

Term	Definition	Examples
verb	The surest way to identify verbs is by the ways they can be used: they can usually have a <u>tense</u>, either <u>present</u> or <u>past</u> (see also <u>future</u>). Verbs are sometimes called 'doing words' because many verbs name an action that someone does; while this can be a way of recognising verbs, it doesn't distinguish verbs from <u>nouns</u> (which can also name actions). Moreover many verbs name states or feelings rather than actions. Verbs can be classified in various ways: for example, as <u>auxiliary</u>, or <u>modal</u>; as <u>transitive</u> or <u>intransitive</u>; and as states or events.	*He* <u>*lives*</u> *in Birmingham.* [present tense] *The teacher* <u>*wrote*</u> *a song for the class.* [past tense] *He* <u>*likes*</u> *chocolate.* [present tense; not an action] *He* <u>*knew*</u> *my father.* [past tense; not an action] Not verbs: *The* <u>*walk*</u> *to Halina's house will take an hour.* [noun] *All that* <u>*surfing*</u> *makes Morwenna so sleepy!* [noun]
vowel	A vowel is a speech sound which is produced without any closure or obstruction of the vocal tract. Vowels can form <u>syllables</u> by themselves, or they may combine with <u>consonants</u>. In the English writing system, the letters *a, e, i, o, u* and *y* can represent vowels.	
word	A word is a unit of grammar: it can be selected and moved around relatively independently, but cannot easily be split. In punctuation, words are normally separated by word spaces. Sometimes, a sequence that appears grammatically to be two words is collapsed into a single written word, indicated with a hyphen or apostrophe (eg *well-built, he's*).	<u>*headteacher*</u> or <u>*head teacher*</u> [can be written with or without a space] <u>*primary-school teacher*</u> [normally written with a hyphen] <u>*I'm*</u> going out. <u>*9.30am*</u>
word class	Every <u>word</u> belongs to a word class which summarises the ways in which it can be used in grammar. The major word classes for English are: <u>noun</u>, <u>verb</u>, <u>adjective</u>, <u>adverb</u>, <u>preposition</u>, <u>determiner</u>, <u>pronoun</u>, <u>conjunction</u>. Word classes are sometimes called 'parts of speech'.	
word family	The <u>words</u> in a word family are normally related to each other by a combination of <u>morphology</u>, grammar and meaning.	<u>*teach – teacher*</u> <u>*extend – extent – extensive*</u> <u>*grammar – grammatical – grammarian*</u>

WHAT'S NEW
IN THE 2014 CURRICULUM?

- Curriculum aims for children to become fluent, reason mathematically and solve problems
- Year-by-year approach to the Curriculum
- Additional stretch in the curriculum, e.g. Algebra in Year 6, recall of multiplication and division facts for multiplication tables up to 12 x 12
- Changes of approach to calculation including new 'Examples of formal written methods of multiplication and division' Appendix (pages 106 - 107)

Scholastic resources that support the 2014 Mathematics Curriculum

100 Maths Lessons

100 Maths Lessons for the 2014 Curriculum brings you a whole year of inspirational, ready-made lessons fully matched to the new curriculum.

- Master the new curriculum: every lesson is carefully matched to the new objectives
- A whole year planned and ready to teach
- Time-saving pick-up-and-use format
- A trusted series: over a million copies sold

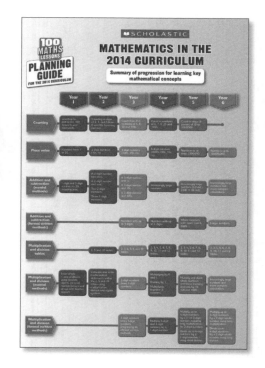

SCHOLASTIC

REAL-LIFE MATHS

Real-Life Maths

Show how maths works in the real world with an innovative approach that brings mathematics to life in the classroom and beyond.

- Role play scenarios encourage active learning
- Facilitates mathematical reasoning and allows children to connect mathematical ideas to solve problems
- Covers key mathematical areas such as number and place value, measurement and times tables
- Enables children to apply mathematical knowledge to other subjects

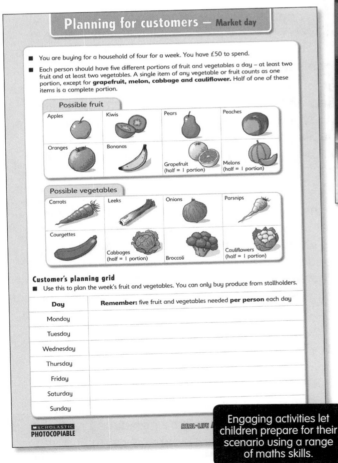

Engaging activities let children prepare for their scenario using a range of maths skills.

Order online at www.scholastic.co.uk/education or phone 0845 603 9091.

Mathematics

Purpose of study

Mathematics is a creative and highly interconnected discipline that has been developed over centuries, providing the solution to some of history's most intriguing problems. It is essential to everyday life, critical to science, technology and engineering, and necessary for financial literacy and most forms of employment. A high-quality mathematics education therefore provides a foundation for understanding the world, the ability to reason mathematically, an appreciation of the beauty and power of mathematics, and a sense of enjoyment and curiosity about the subject.

Aims

The National Curriculum for mathematics aims to ensure that all pupils:

- become **fluent** in the fundamentals of mathematics, including through varied and frequent practice with increasingly complex problems over time, so that pupils have conceptual understanding and are able to recall and apply their knowledge rapidly and accurately
- **reason mathematically** by following a line of enquiry, conjecturing relationships and generalisations, and developing an argument, justification or proof using mathematical language
- can **solve problems** by applying their mathematics to a variety of routine and non-routine problems with increasing sophistication, including breaking down problems into a series of simpler steps and persevering in seeking solutions

Mathematics is an interconnected subject in which pupils need to be able to move fluently between representations of mathematical ideas. The Programmes of Study are, by necessity, organised into apparently distinct domains, but pupils should make rich connections across mathematical ideas to develop fluency, mathematical reasoning and competence in solving increasingly sophisticated problems. They should also apply their mathematical knowledge to science and other subjects.

The expectation is that the majority of pupils will move through the Programmes of Study at broadly the same pace. However, decisions about when to progress should always be based on the security of pupils' understanding and their readiness to progress to the next stage. Pupils who grasp concepts rapidly should be challenged through being offered rich and sophisticated problems before any acceleration through new content. Those who are not sufficiently fluent with earlier material should consolidate their understanding, including through additional practice, before moving on.

Information and communication technology (ICT)

Calculators should not be used as a substitute for good written and mental arithmetic. They should therefore only be introduced near the end of Key Stage 2 to support pupils' conceptual understanding and exploration of more complex number problems, if written and mental arithmetic are secure. In both primary and secondary schools, teachers should use their judgement about when ICT tools should be used.

Spoken language

The National Curriculum for mathematics reflects the importance of spoken language in pupils' development across the whole curriculum – cognitively, socially and linguistically. The quality and variety of language that pupils hear and speak are key factors in developing their mathematical vocabulary and presenting a mathematical justification, argument or proof. They must be assisted in making their thinking clear to themselves as well as others, and teachers should ensure that pupils build secure foundations by using discussion to probe and remedy their misconceptions.

School curriculum

The Programmes of Study for mathematics are set out year-by-year for Key Stages 1 and 2. Schools are, however, only required to teach the relevant Programme of Study by the end of the key stage. Within each key stage, schools therefore have the flexibility to introduce content earlier or later than set out in the Programme of Study. In addition, schools can introduce key stage content during an earlier key stage, if appropriate. All schools are also required to set out their school curriculum for mathematics on a year-by-year basis and make this information available online.

Attainment targets

By the end of each key stage, pupils are expected to know, apply and understand the matters, skills and processes specified in the relevant Programme of Study.

Schools are not required by law to teach the example content in grey tint or the content indicated as being non-statutory.

Key Stage 1 - Years 1 and 2

The principal focus of mathematics teaching in Key Stage 1 is to ensure that pupils develop confidence and mental fluency with whole numbers, counting and place value. This should involve working with numerals, words and the four operations, including with practical resources (for example, concrete objects and measuring tools).

At this stage, pupils should develop their ability to recognise, describe, draw, compare and sort different shapes and use the related vocabulary. Teaching should also involve using a range of measures to describe and compare different quantities such as length, mass, capacity/volume, time and money.

By the end of Year 2, pupils should know the number bonds to 20 and be precise in using and understanding place value. An emphasis on practice at this early stage will aid fluency.

Pupils should read and spell mathematical vocabulary, at a level consistent with their increasing word reading and spelling knowledge at Key Stage 1.

Year 1

Year 1 Programme of Study (statutory requirements)	Notes and guidance (non-statutory)
NUMBER **Number and place value** Pupils should be taught to: • count to and across 100, forwards and backwards, beginning with 0 or 1, or from any given number • count, read and write numbers to 100 in numerals; count in multiples of twos, fives and tens • given a number, identify one more and one less • identify and represent numbers using objects and pictorial representations including the number line, and use the language of: equal to, more than, less than (fewer), most, least • read and write numbers from 1 to 20 in numerals and words.	**NUMBER** **Number and place value** Pupils practise counting (1, 2, 3), ordering (eg first, second, third), or to indicate a quantity (eg 3 apples, 2 centimetres), including solving simple concrete problems, until they are fluent. Pupils begin to recognise place value in numbers beyond 20 by reading, writing, counting and comparing numbers up to 100, supported by objects and pictorial representations. They practise counting as reciting numbers and counting as enumerating objects, and counting in twos, fives and tens from different multiples to develop their recognition of patterns in the number system (eg odd and even numbers), including varied and frequent practice through increasingly complex questions. They recognise and create repeating patterns with objects and with shapes.
Number: Addition and subtraction Pupils should be taught to: • read, write and interpret mathematical statements involving addition (+), subtraction (−) and equals (=) signs • represent and use number bonds and related subtraction facts within 20 • add and subtract one-digit and two-digit numbers to 20, including zero • solve one-step problems that involve addition and subtraction, using concrete objects and pictorial representations, and missing number problems such as $7 = \square - 9$.	**Addition and subtraction** Pupils memorise and reason with number bonds to 10 and 20 in several forms (eg $9 + 7 = 16$; $16 - 7 = 9$; $7 = 16 - 9$). They should realise the effect of adding or subtracting zero. This establishes addition and subtraction as related operations. Pupils combine and increase numbers, counting forwards and backwards. They discuss and solve problems in familiar practical contexts, including using quantities. Problems should include the terms put together, add, altogether, total, take away, distance between, more than and less than, so that pupils develop the concept of addition and subtraction and are enabled to use these operations flexibly.

Year 1 Programme of Study (statutory requirements)	Notes and guidance (non-statutory)
Number: Multiplication and division Pupils should be taught to: • solve one-step problems involving multiplication and division, by calculating the answer using concrete objects, pictorial representations and arrays with the support of the teacher.	**Multiplication and division** Through grouping and sharing small quantities, pupils begin to understand: multiplication and division; doubling numbers and quantities; and finding simple fractions of objects, numbers and quantities. They make connections between arrays, number patterns, and counting in twos, fives and tens.
Fractions Pupils should be taught to: • recognise, find and name a half as one of two equal parts of an object, shape or quantity • recognise, find and name a quarter as one of four equal parts of an object, shape or quantity.	**Fractions** Pupils are taught half and quarter as 'fractions of' discrete and continuous quantities by solving problems using shapes, objects and quantities. For example, they could recognise and find half a length, quantity, set of objects or shape. Pupils connect halves and quarters to the equal sharing and grouping of sets of objects and to measures, as well as recognising and combining halves and quarters as parts of a whole.
MEASUREMENT Pupils should be taught to: • compare, describe and solve practical problems for: • lengths and heights (for example, long/short, longer/shorter, tall/short, double/half) • mass or weight (for example, heavy/light, heavier than, lighter than) • capacity and volume (for example, full/empty, more than, less than, quarter) • time (for example, quicker, slower, earlier, later) • measure and begin to record the following: • lengths and heights • mass/weight • capacity and volume • time (hours, minutes, seconds) • recognise and know the value of different denominations of coins and notes	**MEASUREMENT** The pairs of terms: mass and weight, volume and capacity, are used interchangeably at this stage. Pupils move from using and comparing different types of quantities and measures using non-standard units, including discrete (eg counting) and continuous (eg liquid) measurement, to using manageable common standard units. In order to become familiar with standard measures, pupils begin to use measuring tools such as a ruler, weighing scales and containers. Pupils use the language of time, including telling the time throughout the day, first using o'clock and then half past.

Year 1 Programme of Study (statutory requirements)	Notes and guidance (non-statutory)
• sequence events in chronological order using language for example, before and after, next, first, today, yesterday, tomorrow, morning, afternoon and evening • recognise and use language relating to dates, including days of the week, weeks, months and years • tell the time to the hour and half past the hour and draw the hands on a clock face to show these times.	

GEOMETRY
Properties of shapes
 	
Pupils should be taught to:
 	
• recognise and name common 2D and 3D shapes, including:
 	
  • 2D shapes (for example, rectangles (including squares), circles and triangles)
 	
  • 3D shapes (for example, cuboids (including cubes), pyramids and spheres).
	GEOMETRY
	Properties of shapes
	
	Pupils handle common 2D and 3D shapes, naming these and related everyday objects fluently. They recognise these shapes in different orientations and sizes, and know that rectangles, triangles, cuboids and pyramids are not always similar to each other.

Geometry: Position and direction Pupils should be taught to: • describe position, directions and movements, including half, quarter and three-quarter turns.	**Position and direction** Pupils use the language of position, direction and motion, including: left and right, top, middle and bottom, on top of, in front of, above, between, around, near, close and far, up and down, forwards and backwards, inside and outside. Pupils make whole, half, quarter and three-quarter turns in both directions and connect turning clockwise with movement on a clock face.

Year 2

Year 2 Programme of Study (statutory requirements)	Notes and Guidance (non-statutory)
NUMBER	**NUMBER**
Number and place value	**Number and place value**
Pupils should be taught to:	Using materials and a range of representations, pupils practise counting, reading, writing and comparing numbers to at least 100 and solving a variety of related problems to develop fluency. They count in multiples of three to support their later understanding of a third.
• count in steps of 2, 3 and 5 from 0, and in tens from any number, forward or backward	
• recognise the place value of each digit in a two-digit number (tens, ones)	As they become more confident with numbers up to 100, pupils are introduced to larger numbers to develop further their recognition of patterns within the number system and represent them in different ways, including spatial representations.
• identify, represent and estimate numbers using different representations, including the number line	
• compare and order numbers from 0 up to 100; use <, > and = signs	Pupils should partition numbers in different ways (for example, 23 = 20 + 3 and 23 = 10 + 13) to support subtraction. They become fluent and apply their knowledge of numbers to reason with, discuss and solve problems that emphasise the value of each digit in two-digit numbers. They begin to understand zero as a placeholder.
• read and write numbers to at least 100 in numerals and in words	
• use place value and number facts to solve problems.	
Number: Addition and subtraction	**Addition and subtraction**
Pupils should be taught to:	Pupils extend their understanding of the language of addition and subtraction to include sum and difference.
• solve problems with addition and subtraction:	
• using concrete objects and pictorial representations, including those involving numbers, quantities and measures	Pupils practise addition and subtraction to 20 to become increasingly fluent in deriving facts, such as using 3 + 7 = 10, 10 − 7 = 3 and 7 = 10 − 3 to calculate 30 + 70 = 100, 100 − 70 = 30 and 70 = 100 − 30.
• applying their increasing knowledge of mental and written methods	They check their calculations, including by adding to check subtraction and adding numbers in a different order to check addition (for example, 5 + 2 + 1 = 1 + 5 + 2 = 1 + 2 + 5). This establishes commutativity and associativity of addition.
• recall and use addition and subtraction facts to 20 fluently, and derive and use related facts up to 100	
• add and subtract numbers using concrete objects, pictorial representations, and mentally, including:	Recording addition and subtraction in columns supports place value and prepares for formal written methods with larger numbers.
• a two-digit number and ones	
• a two-digit number and tens	
• two two-digit numbers	
• adding three one-digit numbers	

Year 2 Programme of Study (statutory requirements)

- show that addition of two numbers can be done in any order (commutative) and subtraction of one number from another cannot

- recognise and use the inverse relationship between addition and subtraction and use this to check calculations and missing number problems.

Number: Multiplication and division

Pupils should be taught to:

- recall and use multiplication and division facts for the 2, 5 and 10 multiplication tables, including recognising odd and even numbers

- calculate mathematical statements for multiplication and division within the multiplication tables and write them using the multiplication (×), division (÷) and equals (=) signs

- show that multiplication of two numbers can be done in any order (commutative) and division of one number by another cannot

- solve problems involving multiplication and division, using materials, arrays, repeated addition, mental methods, and multiplication and division facts, including problems in contexts.

Number: Fractions

Pupils should be taught to:

- recognise, find, name and write fractions $\frac{1}{3}$, $\frac{1}{4}$, $\frac{2}{4}$ and $\frac{3}{4}$ of a length, shape, set of objects or quantity

- write simple fractions eg $\frac{1}{2}$ of 6 = 3 and recognise the equivalence of $\frac{2}{4}$ and $\frac{1}{2}$.

Notes and Guidance (non-statutory)

Multiplication and division

Pupils use a variety of language to describe multiplication and division.

Pupils are introduced to the multiplication tables. They practise to become fluent in the 2, 5 and 10 multiplication tables and connect them to each other. They connect the 10 multiplication table to place value, and the 5 multiplication table to the divisions on the clock face. They begin to use other multiplication tables and recall multiplication facts, including using related division facts to perform written and mental calculations.

Pupils work with a range of materials and contexts in which multiplication and division relate to grouping and sharing discrete and continuous quantities, and relating these to fractions and measures (for example, 40 ÷ 2 = 20, 20 is a half of 40). They use commutativity and inverse relations to develop multiplicative reasoning (for example, 4 × 5 = 20 and 20 ÷ 5 = 4).

Fractions

Pupils use fractions as 'fractions of' discrete and continuous quantities by solving problems using shapes, objects and quantities. They connect unit fractions to equal sharing and grouping, to numbers when they can be calculated, and to measures, finding fractions of lengths, quantity, a set of objects or shapes. They meet $\frac{3}{4}$ as the first example of a non-unit fraction.

Pupils should count in fractions up to 10, starting from any number and using the $\frac{1}{2}$ and $\frac{2}{4}$ equivalence on the number line (for example, $1\frac{1}{4}$, $1\frac{2}{4}$ (or $1\frac{1}{2}$), $1\frac{3}{4}$, 2). This reinforces the concept of fractions as numbers and that they can add up to more than one.

Year 2 Programme of Study (statutory requirements)	Notes and Guidance (non-statutory)
MEASUREMENT Pupils should be taught to: • choose and use appropriate standard units to estimate and measure length/height in any direction (m/cm); mass (kg/g); temperature (°C); capacity (litres/ml) to the nearest appropriate unit, using rulers, scales, thermometers and measuring vessels • compare and order lengths, mass, volume/capacity and record the results using >, < and = • recognise and use symbols for pounds (£) and pence (p); combine amounts to make a particular value • find different combinations of coins that equal the same amounts of money • solve simple problems in a practical context involving addition and subtraction of money of the same unit, including giving change • compare and sequence intervals of time • tell and write the time to five minutes, including quarter past/to the hour and draw the hands on a clock face to show these times • know the number of minutes in an hour and the number of hours in a day	**MEASUREMENT** Pupils use standard units of measurement with increasing accuracy, using their knowledge of the number system. They use the appropriate language and record using standard abbreviations. Comparing measures includes simple multiples such as 'half as high'; 'twice as wide'. They become fluent in telling the time on analogue clocks and recording it. Pupils become fluent in counting and recognising coins. They read and say amounts of money confidently and use the symbols £ and p accurately, recording pounds and pence separately.
GEOMETRY **Properties of shapes** Pupils should be taught to: • identify and describe the properties of 2D shapes, including the number of sides and symmetry in a vertical line • identify and describe the properties of 3D shapes, including the number of edges, vertices and faces • identify 2D shapes on the surface of 3D shapes, for example a circle on a cylinder and a triangle on a pyramid • compare and sort common 2D and 3D shapes and everyday objects.	**GEOMETRY** **Properties of shapes** Pupils handle and name a wider variety of common 2D and 3D shapes including: quadrilaterals and cuboids, prisms, cones and polygons, and identify the properties of each shape (eg number of sides, number of faces). Pupils identify, compare and sort shapes on the basis of their properties and use vocabulary precisely, such as sides, edges, vertices and faces. Pupils read and write names for shapes that are appropriate for their word reading and spelling. Pupils draw lines and shapes using a straight edge.

Year 2 Programme of Study (statutory requirements)

Geometry: Position and direction

Pupils should be taught to:

- order and arrange combinations of mathematical objects in patterns and sequences

- use mathematical vocabulary to describe position, direction and movement including in a straight line and distinguishing between rotation as a turn and in terms of right angles for quarter, half and three-quarter turns (clockwise and anti-clockwise).

STATISTICS

Pupils should be taught to:

- interpret and construct simple pictograms, tally charts, block diagrams and simple tables

- ask and answer simple questions by counting the number of objects in each category and sorting the categories by quantity

- ask and answer questions about totalling and comparing categorical data.

Notes and Guidance (non-statutory)

Position and direction

Pupils should work with patterns of shapes, including those in different orientations.

Pupils use the concept and language of angles to describe 'turn' by applying rotations, including in practical contexts (for example, pupils themselves moving in turns, giving instructions to other pupils to do so, and programming robots using instructions given in right angles).

STATISTICS

Pupils record, interpret, collate, organise and compare information (for example, using many-to-one correspondence with simple ratios 2, 5, 10).

Lower Key Stage 2 - Years 3 and 4

The principal focus of mathematics teaching in lower Key Stage 2 is to ensure that pupils become increasingly fluent with whole numbers and the four operations, including number facts and the concept of place value. This should ensure that pupils develop efficient written and mental methods and perform calculations accurately with increasingly large whole numbers.

At this stage, pupils should develop their ability to solve a range of problems, including with simple fractions and decimal place value. Teaching should also ensure that pupils draw with increasing accuracy and develop mathematical reasoning so they can analyse shapes and their properties, and confidently describe the relationships between them. It should ensure that they can use measuring instruments with accuracy and make connections between measure and number.

By the end of Year 4, pupils should have memorised their multiplication tables up to and including the 12 multiplication table and show precision and fluency in their work.

Pupils should read and spell mathematical vocabulary correctly and confidently, using their growing word reading knowledge and their knowledge of spelling.

Year 3

Year 3 Programme of Study (statutory requirements)	Notes and guidance (non-statutory)
NUMBER	**NUMBER**
Number and place value	**Number and place value**
Pupils should be taught to:	Pupils now use multiples of 2, 3, 4, 5, 8, 10, 50 and 100.
• count from 0 in multiples of 4, 8, 50 and 100; find 10 or 100 more or less than a given number	They use larger numbers to at least 1000, applying partitioning related to place value using varied and increasingly complex problems, building on work in Year 2 (for example, 146 = 100 and 40 and 6, 146 = 130 and 16).
• recognise the place value of each digit in a three-digit number (hundreds, tens, ones)	Using a variety of representations, including those related to measure, pupils continue to count in ones, tens and hundreds, so that they become fluent in the order and place value of numbers to 1000.
• compare and order numbers up to 1000	
• identify, represent and estimate numbers using different representations	
• read and write numbers up to 1000 in numerals and in words	
• solve number problems and practical problems involving these ideas.	
Number: Addition and subtraction	**Addition and subtraction**
Pupils should be taught to:	Pupils practise solving varied addition and subtraction questions. For mental calculations with two-digit numbers, the answers could exceed 100.
• add and subtract numbers mentally, including:	
• a three-digit number and ones	Pupils use their understanding of place value and partitioning, and practise using columnar addition and subtraction with increasingly large numbers up to three digits to become fluent (see Mathematics Appendix 1).
• a three-digit number and tens	
• a three-digit number and hundreds	
• add and subtract numbers with up to three digits, using formal written methods of columnar addition and subtraction	
• estimate the answer to a calculation and use inverse operations to check answers	
• solve problems, including missing number problems, using number facts, place value, and more complex addition and subtraction.	

Year 3 Programme of Study (statutory requirements)

Number: Multiplication and division

Pupils should be taught to:

- recall and use multiplication and division facts for the 3, 4 and 8 multiplication tables

- write and calculate mathematical statements for multiplication and division using the multiplication tables that they know, including for two-digit numbers times one-digit numbers, using mental methods and progressing to formal written methods

- solve problems, including missing number problems, involving multiplication and division, including integer scaling problems and correspondence problems in which *n* objects are connected to *m* objects.

Notes and guidance (non-statutory)

Multiplication and division

Pupils continue to practise their mental recall of multiplication tables when they are calculating mathematical statements in order to improve fluency. Through doubling, they connect the 2, 4 and 8 multiplication tables.

Pupils develop efficient mental methods, for example, using commutativity and associativity (for example, $4 \times 12 \times 5 = 4 \times 5 \times 12 = 20 \times 12 = 240$) and multiplication and division facts (for example, using $3 \times 2 = 6$, $6 \div 3 = 2$ and $2 = 6 \div 3$) to derive related facts (for example, $30 \times 2 = 60$, $60 \div 3 = 20$ and $20 = 60 \div 3$).

Pupils develop reliable written methods for multiplication and division, starting with calculations of two-digit numbers by one-digit numbers and progressing to the formal written methods of short multiplication and division.

Pupils solve simple problems in contexts, deciding which of the four operations to use and why. These include measuring and scaling contexts, (for example, four times as high, eight times as long etc.) and correspondence problems in which *m* objects are connected to *n* objects (for example, 3 hats and 4 coats – how many different outfits?; 12 sweets shared equally between 4 children; 4 cakes shared equally between 8 children).

Year 3 Programme of Study (statutory requirements)

Number: Fractions

Pupils should be taught to:

- count up and down in tenths; recognise that tenths arise from dividing an object into 10 equal parts and in dividing one-digit numbers or quantities by 10
- recognise, find and write fractions of a discrete set of objects: unit fractions and non-unit fractions with small denominators
- recognise and use fractions as numbers: unit fractions and non-unit fractions with small denominators
- recognise and show, using diagrams, equivalent fractions with small denominators
- add and subtract fractions with the same denominator within one whole (for example, $5/7 + 1/7 = 6/7$)
- compare and order unit fractions, and fractions with the same denominators
- solve problems that involve all of the above.

MEASUREMENT

Pupils should be taught to:

- measure, compare, add and subtract: lengths (m/cm/mm); mass (kg/g); volume/capacity (l/ml)
- measure the perimeter of simple 2D shapes
- add and subtract amounts of money to give change, using both £ and p in practical contexts
- tell and write the time from an analogue clock, including using Roman numerals from I to XII, and 12-hour and 24-hour clocks
- estimate and read time with increasing accuracy to the nearest minute; record and compare time in terms of seconds, minutes, hours and o'clock; use vocabulary such as a.m./p.m., morning, afternoon, noon and midnight
- know the number of seconds in a minute and the number of days in each month, year and leap year
- compare durations of events, for example to calculate the time taken by particular events or tasks.

Notes and guidance (non-statutory)

Fractions

Pupils connect tenths to place value, decimal measures and to division by 10.

They begin to understand unit and non-unit fractions as numbers on the number line, and deduce relations between them, such as size and equivalence. They should go beyond the [0, 1] interval, relating this to measure.

Pupils understand the relation between unit fractions as operators (fractions of), and division by integers.

They continue to recognise fractions in the context of parts of a whole, numbers, measurements, a shape, and unit fractions as a division of a quantity.

Pupils practise adding and subtracting fractions with the same denominator through a variety of increasingly complex problems to improve fluency.

MEASUREMENT

Pupils continue to measure using the appropriate tools and units, progressing to using a wider range of measures, including comparing and using mixed units (for example, 1kg and 200g) and simple equivalents of mixed units (for example, 5m = 500cm).

The comparison of measures should also include simple scaling by integers (for example, a given quantity or measure is twice as long or five times as high) and this should connect to multiplication.

Pupils continue to become fluent in recognising the value of coins, by adding and subtracting amounts, including mixed units, and giving change using manageable amounts. They record £ and p separately. The decimal recording of money is introduced formally in Year 4.

Pupils use both analogue and digital 12-hour clocks and record their times. In this way they become fluent in and prepared for using digital 24-hour clocks in Year 4.

Year 3 Programme of Study (statutory requirements)	Notes and guidance (non-statutory)
GEOMETRY **Properties of shapes** Pupils should be taught to: • draw 2D shapes and make 3D shapes using modelling materials; recognise 3D shapes in different orientations and describe them • recognise angles as a property of shape or a description of a turn • identify right angles, recognise that two right angles make a half-turn, three make three quarters of a turn and four a complete turn; identify whether angles are greater than or less than a right angle • identify horizontal and vertical lines and pairs of perpendicular and parallel lines.	**GEOMETRY** **Properties of shapes** Pupils' knowledge of the properties of shapes is extended at this stage to symmetrical and non-symmetrical polygons and polyhedra. Pupils extend their use of the properties of shapes. They should be able to describe the properties of 2D and 3D shapes using accurate language, including lengths of lines and acute and obtuse for angles greater or lesser than a right angle. Pupils connect decimals and rounding to drawing and measuring straight lines in centimetres, in a variety of contexts.
STATISTICS Pupils should be taught to: • interpret and present data using bar charts, pictograms and tables • solve one-step and two-step questions (for example 'How many more?' and 'How many fewer?') using information presented in scaled bar charts and pictograms and tables.	**STATISTICS** Pupils understand and use simple scales (for example, 2, 5, 10 units per cm) in pictograms and bar charts with increasing accuracy. They continue to interpret data presented in many contexts.

Year 4

Year 4 Programme of Study (statutory requirements)	Notes and guidance (non-statutory)
NUMBER	**NUMBER**
Number and place value	**Number and place value**
Pupils should be taught to:	Using a variety of representations, including measures, pupils become fluent in the order and place value of numbers beyond 1000, including counting in tens and hundreds, and maintaining fluency in other multiples through varied and frequent practice.
• count in multiples of 6, 7, 9, 25 and 1000	
• find 1000 more or less than a given number	
• count backwards through zero to include negative numbers	They begin to extend their knowledge of the number system to include the decimal numbers and fractions that they have met so far.
• recognise the place value of each digit in a four-digit number (thousands, hundreds, tens and ones)	They connect estimation and rounding numbers to the use of measuring instruments.
• order and compare numbers beyond 1000	
• identify, represent and estimate numbers using different representations	Roman numerals should be put in their historical context so pupils understand that there have been different ways to write whole numbers and that the important concepts of zero and place value were introduced over a period of time.
• round any number to the nearest 10, 100 or 1000	
• solve number and practical problems that involve all of the above and with increasingly large positive numbers	
• read Roman numerals to 100 (I to C) and know that over time, the numeral system changed to include the concept of zero and place value.	
Number: Addition and subtraction	**Addition and subtraction**
Pupils should be taught to:	Pupils continue to practise both mental methods and columnar addition and subtraction with increasingly large numbers to aid fluency (see Mathematics Appendix 1).
• add and subtract numbers with up to 4 digits using the formal written methods of columnar addition and subtraction where appropriate	
• estimate and use inverse operations to check answers to a calculation	
• solve addition and subtraction two-step problems in contexts, deciding which operations and methods to use and why.	

Year 4 Programme of Study (statutory requirements)

Number: Multiplication and division

Pupils should be taught to:

- recall multiplication and division facts for multiplication tables up to 12 × 12

- use place value, known and derived facts to multiply and divide mentally, including: multiplying by 0 and 1; dividing by 1; multiplying together three numbers

- recognise and use factor pairs and commutativity in mental calculations

- multiply two-digit and three-digit numbers by a one-digit number using formal written layout

- solve problems involving multiplying and adding, including using the distributive law to multiply two-digit numbers by one digit, integer scaling problems and harder correspondence problems such as *n* objects are connected to *m* objects.

Notes and guidance (non-statutory)

Multiplication and division

Pupils continue to practise recalling and using multiplication tables and related division facts to aid fluency.

Pupils practise mental methods and extend this to three-digit numbers to derive facts (for example $600 \div 3 = 200$ can be derived from $2 \times 3 = 6$)

Pupils practise to become fluent in the formal written method of short multiplication for multiplying using multi-digit numbers, and short division with exact answers when dividing by a one-digit number (see Mathematics Appendix 1).

Pupils write statements about the equality of expressions (for example, use the distributive law $39 \times 7 = 30 \times 7 + 9 \times 7$ and associative law ($2 \times 3) \times 4 = 2 \times (3 \times 4)$). They combine their knowledge of number facts and rules of arithmetic to solve mental and written calculations for example, $2 \times 6 \times 5 = 10 \times 6$.

Pupils solve two-step problems in contexts, choosing the appropriate operation, working with increasingly harder numbers. This should include correspondence questions such as the numbers of choices of a meal on a menu, or three cakes shared equally between 10 children.

Year 4 Programme of Study (statutory requirements)	Notes and guidance (non-statutory)
Number: Fractions (including decimals)	**Fractions (including decimals)**
Pupils should be taught to:	Pupils should connect hundredths to tenths and place value and decimal measure.
• recognise and show, using diagrams, families of common equivalent fractions	They extend the use of the number line to connect fractions, numbers and measures.
• count up and down in hundredths; recognise that hundredths arise when dividing an object by a hundred and dividing tenths by ten.	Pupils understand the relation between non-unit fractions and multiplication and division of quantities, with particular emphasis on tenths and hundredths.
• solve problems involving increasingly harder fractions to calculate quantities, and fractions to divide quantities, including non-unit fractions where the answer is a whole number	Pupils make connections between fractions of a length, of a shape and as a representation of one whole or set of quantities. Pupils use factors and multiples to recognise equivalent fractions and simplify where appropriate (for example, $^6/_9 = {^2/_3}$ or $^1/_4 = {^2/_8}$).
• add and subtract fractions with the same denominator	Pupils continue to practise adding and subtracting fractions with the same denominator, to become fluent through a variety of increasingly complex problems beyond one whole.
• recognise and write decimal equivalents of any number of tenths or hundredths	Pupils are taught throughout that decimals and fractions are different ways of expressing numbers and proportions.
• recognise and write decimal equivalents to $^1/_4$; $^1/_2$; $^3/_4$	Pupils' understanding of the number system and decimal place value is extended at this stage to tenths and then hundredths. This includes relating the decimal notation to division of whole number by 10 and later 100.
• find the effect of dividing a one- or two-digit number by 10 and 100, identifying the value of the digits in the answer as units, tenths and hundredths	They practise counting using simple fractions and decimal fractions, both forwards and backwards.
• round decimals with one decimal place to the nearest whole number	Pupils learn decimal notation and the language associated with it, including in the context of measurements. They make comparisons and order decimal amounts and quantities that are expressed to the same number of decimal places. They should be able to represent numbers with one or two decimal places in several ways, such as on number lines.
• compare numbers with the same number of decimal places up to two decimal places	
• solve simple measure and money problems involving fractions and decimals to two decimal places.	

Year 4 Programme of Study (statutory requirements)	Notes and guidance (non-statutory)
MEASUREMENT	**MEASUREMENT**
Pupils should be taught to:	Pupils build on their understanding of place value and decimal notation to record metric measures, including money.
• Convert between different units of measure (for example, kilometre to metre; hour to minute)	They use multiplication to convert from larger to smaller units.
• measure and calculate the perimeter of a rectilinear figure (including squares) in centimetres and metres	Perimeter can be expressed algebraically as $2(a + b)$ where a and b are the dimensions in the same unit.
• find the area of rectilinear shapes by counting squares	They relate area to arrays and multiplication.
• estimate, compare and calculate different measures, including money in pounds and pence	
• read, write and convert time between analogue and digital 12- and 24-hour clocks	
• solve problems involving converting from hours to minutes; minutes to seconds; years to months; weeks to days.	
GEOMETRY	**GEOMETRY**
Properties of shapes	**Properties of shapes**
Pupils should be taught to:	Pupils continue to classify shapes using geometrical properties, extending to classifying different triangles (for example, isosceles, equilateral, scalene) and quadrilaterals (for example, parallelogram, rhombus, trapezium).
• compare and classify geometric shapes, including quadrilaterals and triangles, based on their properties and sizes	Pupils compare and order angles in preparation for using a protractor and compare lengths and angles to decide if a polygon is regular or irregular.
• identify acute and obtuse angles and compare and order angles up to two right angles by size	Pupils draw symmetric patterns using a variety of media to become familiar with different orientations of lines of symmetry; and recognise line symmetry in a variety of diagrams, including where the line of symmetry does not dissect the original shape.
• identify lines of symmetry in 2D shapes presented in different orientations	
• complete a simple symmetric figure with respect to a specific line of symmetry.	

Year 4 Programme of Study (statutory requirements)	Notes and guidance (non-statutory)
Geometry: Position and direction Pupils should be taught to: • describe positions on a 2D grid as coordinates in the first quadrant • describe movements between positions as translations of a given unit to the left/right and up/down • plot specified points and draw sides to complete a given polygon.	**Position and direction** Pupils draw a pair of axes in one quadrant, with equal scales and integer labels. They read, write and use pairs of coordinates for example (2, 5) including using coordinate-plotting ICT tools.
STATISTICS Pupils should be taught to: • interpret and present discrete and continuous data using appropriate graphical methods, including bar charts and time graphs • solve comparison, sum and difference problems using information presented in bar charts, pictograms, tables and other graphs.	**STATISTICS** Pupils understand and use a greater range of scales in their representations. Pupils begin to relate the graphical representation of data to recording change over time.

Upper Key Stage 2 - Years 5 and 6

The principal focus of mathematics teaching in upper Key Stage 2 is to ensure that pupils extend their understanding of the number system and place value to include larger integers. This should develop the connections that pupils make between multiplication and division with fractions, decimals, percentages and ratio.

At this stage, pupils should develop their ability to solve a wider range of problems, including increasingly complex properties of numbers and arithmetic, and problems demanding efficient written and mental methods of calculation. With this foundation in arithmetic, pupils are introduced to the language of algebra as a means for solving a variety of problems. Teaching in geometry and measures should consolidate and extend knowledge developed in number. Teaching should also ensure that pupils classify shapes with increasingly complex geometric properties and that they learn the vocabulary they need to describe them.

By the end of Year 6, pupils should be fluent in written methods for all four operations, including long multiplication and division, and in working with fractions, decimals and percentages.

Pupils should read, spell and pronounce mathematical vocabulary correctly.

Year 5

Year 5 Programme of Study (statutory requirements)	Notes and guidance (non-statutory)
NUMBER **Number and place value** Pupils should be taught to: • read, write, order and compare numbers to at least 1,000,000 and determine the value of each digit • count forwards or backwards in steps of powers of 10 for any given number up to 1,000,000 • interpret negative numbers in context, count forwards and backwards with positive and negative whole numbers through zero • round any number up to 1,000,000 to the nearest 10, 100, 1000, 10,000 and 100,000 • solve number problems and practical problems that involve all of the above • read Roman numerals to 1000 (M) and recognise years written in Roman numerals.	**NUMBER** **Number and place value** Pupils identify the place value in large whole numbers. They continue to use number in context, including measurement. Pupils extend and apply their understanding of the number system to the decimal numbers and fractions that they have met so far. They should recognise and describe linear number sequences, including those involving fractions and decimals, and find the term-to-term rule. They should recognise and describe linear number sequences (for example, 3, $3\frac{1}{2}$, 4, $4\frac{1}{2}$ ...), including those involving fractions and decimals, and find the term-to-term rule in words (for example, add $\frac{1}{2}$).
Number: Addition and subtraction Pupils should be taught to: • add and subtract whole numbers with more than 4 digits, including using formal written methods (columnar addition and subtraction) • add and subtract numbers mentally with increasingly large numbers • use rounding to check answers to calculations and determine, in the context of a problem, levels of accuracy • solve addition and subtraction multi-step problems in contexts, deciding which operations and methods to use and why.	**Addition and subtraction** Pupils practise using the formal written methods of columnar addition and subtraction with increasingly large numbers to aid fluency (see Mathematics Appendix 1). They practise mental calculations with increasingly large numbers to aid fluency (for example, 12,462 – 2300 = 10,162).

Year 5 Programme of Study (statutory requirements)	Notes and guidance (non-statutory)
Number: Multiplication and division Pupils should be taught to: • identify multiples and factors, including finding all factor pairs of a number, and common factors of two numbers. • know and use the vocabulary of prime numbers, prime factors and composite (non-prime) numbers • establish whether a number up to 100 is prime and recall prime numbers up to 19 • multiply numbers up to 4 digits by a one- or two-digit number using a formal written method, including long multiplication for two-digit numbers • multiply and divide numbers mentally drawing upon known facts • divide numbers up to 4 digits by a one-digit number using the formal written method of short division and interpret remainders appropriately for the context • multiply and divide whole numbers and those involving decimals by 10, 100 and 1000 • recognise and use square numbers and cube numbers, and the notation for squared (^{2}) and cubed (^{3}) • solve problems involving multiplication and division including using their knowledge of factors and multiples, squares and cubes • solve problems involving addition, subtraction, multiplication and division and a combination of these, including understanding the meaning of the equals sign • solve problems involving multiplication and division, including scaling by simple fractions and problems involving simple rates.	**Multiplication and division** Pupils practise and extend their use of the formal written methods of short multiplication and short division (see Mathematics Appendix 1). They apply all the multiplication tables and related division facts frequently, commit them to memory and use them confidently to make larger calculations. They use and understand the terms factor, multiple and prime, square and cube numbers. Pupils interpret non-integer answers to division by expressing results in different ways according to the context, including with remainders, as fractions, as decimals or by rounding (eg $98 \div 4 = 24$ r $2 = 24^1/_2 = 24.5 \approx 25$). Pupils use multiplication and division as inverses to support the introduction of ratio in Year 6, for example, by multiplying and dividing by powers of 10 in scale drawings or by multiplying and dividing by powers of 1000 in converting between units such as kilometres and metres. Distributivity can be expressed as $a(b + c) = ab + ac$. They understand the terms factor, multiple and prime, squre and cube numbers and use them to construct equivalence statements (for example, $4 \times 35 = 2 \times 2 \times 35$; $3 \times 270 = 3 \times 3 \times 9 \times 10 = 9^2 \times 10$) Pupils use and explain the equals sign to indicate, equivalence, including missing number problems (for example, $13 + 24 = 12 + 25$; $33 = 5 \times \square$).

Year 5 Programme of Study (statutory requirements)	Notes and guidance (non-statutory)
Number: Fractions (including decimals and percentages)	**Fractions (including decimals and percentages)**
Pupils should be taught to:	Pupils should be taught throughout that percentages, decimals and fractions are different ways of expressing proportions.
• compare and order fractions whose denominators are all multiples of the same number	They extend their knowledge of fractions to thousandths and connect to decimals and measures.
• identify, name and write equivalent fractions of a given fraction, represented visually, including tenths and hundredths	Pupils connect equivalent fractions > 1 to division with remainders, using the number line and other models, and hence move from these to improper and mixed fractions.
• recognise mixed numbers and improper fractions and convert from one form to the other and write mathematical statements > 1 as a mixed number (for example, $2/5 + 4/5 = 6/5 = 1^1/5$)	
• add and subtract fractions with the same denominator and multiples of the same number	Pupils connect multiplication by a fraction to using fractions as operators (fractions of), and to division, building on work from previous years. This relates to scaling by simple fractions, including fractions > 1.
• multiply proper fractions and mixed numbers by whole numbers, supported by materials and diagrams	Pupils practise adding and subtracting fractions to become fluent through a variety of increasingly complex problems. They extend their understanding of adding and subtracting fractions to calculations that exceed 1 as a mixed number.
• read and write decimal numbers as fractions (for example, 0.71 = $71/100$)	
• recognise and use thousandths and relate them to tenths, hundredths and decimal equivalents	Pupils continue to practise counting forwards and backwards in simple fractions.
• round decimals with two decimal places to the nearest whole number and to one decimal place	Pupils continue to develop their understanding of fractions as numbers, measures and operators by finding fractions of numbers and quantities.
• read, write, order and compare numbers with up to three decimal places	Pupils extend counting from Year 4, using decimals and fractions including bridging zero, for example on a number line.
• solve problems involving numbers up to three decimal places	Pupils say, read and write decimal fractions and related tenths, hundredths and thousandths accurately and are confident in checking the reasonableness of their answers to problems.
• recognise the per cent symbol (%) and understand that per cent relates to 'number of parts per hundred', and write percentages as a fraction with denominator hundred, and as a decimal	They mentally add and subtract tenths, and one-digit whole numbers and tenths.
• solve problems which require knowing percentage and decimal equivalents of $1/2$, $1/4$, $1/5$, $2/5$, $4/5$ and those fractions with a denominator of a multiple of 10 or 25.	

Year 5 Programme of Study (statutory requirements)	Notes and guidance (non-statutory)
	They practise adding and subtracting decimals, including a mix of whole numbers and decimals, decimals with different numbers of decimal places, and complements of 1 (for example, 0.83 + 0.17 = 1).

Pupils should go beyond the measurement and money models of decimals, for example by solving puzzles involving decimals.

Pupils should make connections between percentages, fractions and decimals (for example, 100% represents a whole quantity and 1% is $^1/_{100}$, 50% is $^{50}/_{100}$, 25% is $^{25}/_{100}$) and relate this to finding 'fractions of'. |
| **MEASUREMENT**

Pupils should be taught to:

• convert between different units of metric measure (for example, kilometre and metre; centimetre and metre; centimetre and millimetre; gram and kilogram; litre and millilitre)

• understand and use equivalences between metric units and common imperial units such as inches, pounds and pints

• measure and calculate the perimeter of composite rectilinear shapes in centimetres and metres

• calculate and compare the area of rectangles (including squares), and including using standard units, square centimetres (cm^2) and square metres (m^2) and estimate the area of irregular shapes

• estimate volume (for example, using 1cm^3 blocks to build cubes and cuboids) and capacity (for example, using water)

• solve problems involving converting between units of time

• use all four operations to solve problems involving measure (for example, length, mass, volume, money) using decimal notation including scaling. | **MEASUREMENT**

Pupils use their knowledge of place value and multiplication and division to convert between standard units.

Pupils calculate the perimeter of rectangles and related composite shapes, including using the relations of perimeter or area to find unknown lengths. Missing measures questions such as these can be expressed algebraically, for example 4 + 2b = 20 for a rectangle of sides 2cm and b/cm and perimeter of 20cm.

Pupils calculate the area from scale drawings using given measurements.

Pupils use all four operations in problems involving time and money, including conversions (for example, days to weeks, expressing the answer as weeks and days). |

Year 5 Programme of Study (statutory requirements)

GEOMETRY

Properties of shapes

Pupils should be taught to:

- identify 3D shapes, including cubes and other cuboids, from 2D representations

- know angles are measured in degrees: estimate and compare acute, obtuse and reflex angles

- draw given angles, and measure them in degrees (°)

- identify:
  - angles at a point and one whole turn (total 360°)
  - angles at a point on a straight line and ½ a turn (total 180°)
  - other multiples of 90°

- use the properties of rectangles to deduce related facts and find missing lengths and angles

- distinguish between regular and irregular polygons based on reasoning about equal sides and angles.

Geometry: Position and direction

Pupils should be taught to:

- identify, describe and represent the position of a shape following a reflection or translation, using the appropriate language, and know that the shape has not changed.

STATISTICS

Pupils should be taught to:

- solve comparison, sum and difference problems using information presented in a line graph

- complete, read and interpret information in tables, including timetables.

Notes and guidance (non-statutory)

GEOMETRY

Properties of shapes

Pupils become accurate in drawing lines with a ruler to the nearest millimetre, and measuring with a protractor. They use conventional markings for parallel lines and right angles.

Pupils use the term *diagonal* and make conjectures about the angles formed by diagonals and sides, and other properties of quadrilaterals, for example using dynamic geometry ICT tools.

Pupils use angle sum facts and other properties to make deductions about missing angles and relate these to missing number problems.

Position and direction

Pupils recognise and use reflection and translation in a variety of diagrams, including continuing to use a 2D grid and coordinates in the first quadrant. Reflection should be in lines that are parallel to the axes.

STATISTICS

Pupils connect their work on coordinates and scales to their interpretation of time graphs.

They begin to decide which representations of data are most appropriate and why.

Year 6

Year 6 Programme of Study (statutory requirements)	Notes and guidance (non-statutory)
NUMBER	**NUMBER**
Number and place value	**Number and place value**
Pupils should be taught to:	Pupils use the whole number system, including saying, reading and writing numbers accurately.
• read, write, order and compare numbers up to 10,000,000 and determine the value of each digit	
• round any whole number to a required degree of accuracy	
• use negative numbers in context, and calculate intervals across zero	
• solve number and practical problems that involve all of the above.	
Number: Addition, subtraction, multiplication and division	**Addition, subtraction, multiplication and division**
Pupils should be taught to:	Pupils practise addition, subtraction, multiplication and division for larger numbers, using the formal written methods of columnar addition and subtraction, short and long multiplication, and short and long division (see Mathematics Appendix 1).
• multiply multi-digit numbers up to 4 digits by a two-digit whole number using the formal written method of long multiplication	
• divide numbers up to 4 digits by a two-digit whole number using the formal written method of long division, and interpret remainders as whole number remainders, fractions, or by rounding, as appropriate for the context	They undertake mental calculations with increasingly large numbers and more complex calculations.
• divide numbers up to 4 digits by a two-digit number using the formal written method of short division where appropriate, interpreting remainders according to the context	Pupils continue to use all the multiplication tables to calculate mathematical statements in order to maintain their fluency.
	Pupils round answers to a specified degree of accuracy, eg to the nearest 10, 20, 50 etc, but not to a specified number of significant figures.
• perform mental calculations, including with mixed operations and large numbers.	
• identify common factors, common multiples and prime numbers	Pupils explore the order of operations using brackets; for example, $2 + 1 \times 3 = 5$ and $(2 + 1) \times 3 = 9$.
• use their knowledge of the order of operations to carry out calculations involving the four operations	Common factors can be related to finding equivalent fractions.
• solve addition and subtraction multi-step problems in contexts, deciding which operations and methods to use and why	
• solve problems involving addition, subtraction, multiplication and division	
• use estimation to check answers to calculations and determine, in the context of a problem, an appropriate degree of accuracy.	

Year 6 Programme of Study (statutory requirements)

Number: Fractions (including decimals and percentages)

Pupils should be taught to:

- use common factors to simplify fractions; use common multiples to express fractions in the same denomination

- compare and order fractions, including fractions >1

- add and subtract fractions with different denominators and mixed numbers, using the concept of equivalent fractions

- multiply simple pairs of proper fractions, writing the answer in its simplest form (for example, $\frac{1}{4} \times \frac{1}{2} = \frac{1}{8}$)

- divide proper fractions by whole numbers (for example, $\frac{1}{3} \div 2 = \frac{1}{6}$)

- associate a fraction with division and calculate decimal fraction equivalents (for example, 0.375) for a simple fraction (for example, $\frac{3}{8}$)

- identify the value of each digit in numbers given to three decimal places and multiply and divide numbers by 10, 100 and 1000 giving answers up to three decimal places

- multiply one-digit numbers with up to two decimal places by whole numbers

- use written division methods in cases where the answer has up to two decimal places

- solve problems which require answers to be rounded to specified degrees of accuracy

- recall and use equivalences between simple fractions, decimals and percentages, including in different contexts.

Notes and guidance (non-statutory)

Fractions (including decimals and percentages)

Pupils should practise, use and understand the addition and subtraction of fractions with different denominators by identifying equivalent fractions with the same denominator. They should start with fractions where the denominator of one fraction is a multiple of the other (for example, $\frac{1}{2} + \frac{1}{8} = \frac{5}{8}$) and progress to varied and increasingly complex problems.

Pupils should use a variety of images to support their understanding of multiplication with fractions. This follows earlier work about fractions as operators (fractions of), as numbers, and as equal parts of objects, for example as parts of a rectangle.

Pupils use their understanding of the relationship between unit fractions and division to work backwards by multiplying a quantity that represents a unit fraction to find the whole quantity (for example, if $\frac{1}{4}$ of a length is 36cm, then the whole length is $36 \times 4 = 144$cm).

They practise with simple fractions and decimal fraction equivalents to aid fluency, including listing equivalent fractions to identify fractions with common denominators.

Pupils can explore and make conjectures about converting a simple fraction to a decimal fraction (e.g. $3 \div 8 = 0.375$). For simple fractions with recurring decimal equivalents, pupils learn about rounding the decimal to three decimal places, or other appropriate approximations depending on the context. Pupils multiply and divide numbers with up to two decimal places by one-digit and two-digit whole numbers. Pupils multiply decimals by whole numbers, starting with the simplest cases, such as $0.4 \times 2 = 0.8$, and in practical contexts, such as measures and money.

Pupils are introduced to the division of decimal numbers by one-digit whole numbers and, initially, in practical contexts involving measures and money. They recognise division calculations as the inverse of multiplication.

Pupils also develop their skills of rounding and estimating as a means of predicting and checking the order of magnitude of their answers to decimal calculations. This includes rounding answers to a specified degree of accuracy and checking the reasonableness of their answers.

Year 6 Programme of Study (statutory requirements)	Notes and guidance (non-statutory)
RATIO AND PROPORTION Pupils should be taught to: • solve problems involving the relative sizes of two quantities where missing values can be found by using integer multiplication and division facts • solve problems involving the calculation of percentages (for example, of measures, and such as 15% of 360) and the use of percentages for comparison • solve problems involving similar shapes where the scale factor is known or can be found • solve problems involving unequal sharing and grouping using knowledge of fractions and multiples. **ALGEBRA** Pupils should be taught to: • use simple formulae • generate and describe linear number sequences • express missing number problems algebraically • find pairs of numbers that satisfy an equation with two unknowns • enumerate all possibilities of combinations of two variables.	**RATIO AND PROPORTION** Pupils recognise proportionality in contexts when the relations between quantities are in the same ratio (for example, similar shapes and recipes). Pupils link percentages or 360° to calculating angles of pie charts. Pupils should consolidate their understanding of ratio when comparing quantities, sizes and scale drawings by solving a variety of problems. They might use the notation $a:b$ to record their work. Pupils solve problems involving unequal quantities eg 'for every egg you need three spoonfuls of flour', '$3/5$ of the class are boys'. These problems are the foundation for later formal approaches to ratio and proportion. **ALGEBRA** Pupils should be introduced to the use of symbols and letters to represent variables and unknowns in mathematical situations that they already understand, such as: • missing numbers, lengths, coordinates and angles • formulae in mathematics and science • equivalent expressions (for example, $a + b = b + a$) • generalisations of number patterns • number puzzles (for example, what two numbers can add up to).

SCHOLASTIC

Year 6 Programme of Study (statutory requirements)	Notes and guidance (non-statutory)
MEASUREMENT	**MEASUREMENT**
Pupils should be taught to:	Pupils connect conversion (for example, from kilometres to miles) to a graphical representation as preparation for understanding linear/proportional graphs.
• solve problems involving the calculation and conversion of units of measure, using decimal notation up to three decimal places where appropriate	They know approximate conversions and are able to tell if an answer is sensible.
• use, read, write and convert between standard units, converting measurements of length, mass, volume and time from a smaller unit of measure to a larger unit, and vice versa, using decimal notation to up to three decimal places	Using the number line, pupils use, add and subtract positive and negative integers for measures such as temperature.
• convert between miles and kilometres	They relate the area of rectangles to parallelograms and triangles, for example, by dissection, and calculate their areas, understanding and using the formulae (in words or symbols) to do this.
• recognise that shapes with the same areas can have different perimeters and vice versa	Pupils could be introduced to compound units for speed, such as miles per hour, and apply their knowledge in science or other subjects as appropriate.
• recognise when it is possible to use formulae for area and volume of shapes	
• calculate the area of parallelograms and triangles	
• calculate, estimate and compare volume of cubes and cuboids using standard units, including centimetre cubed (cm^3) and cubic metres (m^3), and extending to other units (for example, mm^3 and km^3).	

Year 6 Programme of Study (statutory requirements)	Notes and guidance (non-statutory)
GEOMETRY **Properties of shapes** Pupils should be taught to: • draw 2D shapes using given dimensions and angles • recognise, describe and build simple 3D shapes, including making nets • compare and classify geometric shapes based on their properties and sizes and find unknown angles in any triangles, quadrilaterals, and regular polygons • illustrate and name parts of circles, including radius, diameter and circumference and know that the diameter is twice the radius • recognise angles where they meet at a point, are on a straight line, or are vertically opposite, and find missing angles.	**GEOMETRY** **Properties of shapes** Pupils draw shapes and nets accurately, using measuring tools and conventional markings and labels for lines and angles. Pupils describe the properties of shapes and explain how unknown angles and lengths can be derived from known measurements. These relationships might be expressed algebraically for example, $d = 2 \times r$, $a = 180 - (b + c)$.
Geometry: Position and direction Pupils should be taught to: • describe positions on the full coordinate grid (all four quadrants) • draw and translate simple shapes on the coordinate plane, and reflect them in the axes.	**Position and direction** Pupils draw and label a pair of axes in all four quadrants with equal scaling. This extends their knowledge of one quadrant to all four quadrants, including the use of negative numbers. Pupils draw and label rectangles (including squares), parallelograms and rhombuses, specified by coordinates in the four quadrants, predicting missing coordinates using the properties of shapes. These might be expressed algebraically for example, translating vertex (a, b) to $(a - 2, b + 3)$; (a, b) and $(a + d, b + d)$ being opposite vertices of a square of side d.
STATISTICS Pupils should be taught to: • interpret and construct pie charts and line graphs and use these to solve problems • calculate and interpret the mean as an average.	**STATISTICS** Pupils connect their work on angles, fractions and percentages to the interpretation of pie charts. Pupils both encounter and draw graphs relating two variables, arising from their own enquiry and in other subjects. They should connect conversion from kilometres to miles in measurement to its graphical representation. Pupils know when it is appropriate to find the mean of a data set.

Mathematics Appendix 1: Examples of formal written methods for addition, subtraction, multiplication and division

This appendix sets out some examples of formal written methods for all four operations to illustrate the range of methods that could be taught. It is not intended to be an exhaustive list, nor is it intended to show progression in formal written methods. For example, the exact position of intermediate calculations (superscript and subscript digits) will vary depending on the method and format used.

For multiplication, some pupils may include an addition symbol when adding partial products. For division, some pupils may include a subtraction symbol when subtracting multiples of the divisor.

Addition and subtraction

789 + 642 becomes

```
      7  8  9
  +   6  4  2
  _____
  1   4  3  1
      1  1
```
Answer: 1431

874 – 523 becomes

```
      8  7  4
  -   5  2  3
  _____
      3  5  1
```
Answer: 351

932 – 457 becomes

```
    8_9  12_3  1_2
  -   4   5    7
  _____
      4   7    5
```
Answer: 475

932 – 457 becomes

```
      9   1_3   1_2
  -  4_5  5_6   7
  _____
      4    7    5
```
Answer: 475

Short multiplication

24 × 6 becomes

```
      2  4
  ×      6
  _____
  1   4  4
      2
```
Answer: 144

342 × 7 becomes

```
      3  4  2
  ×         7
  _____
  2   3  9  4
      2  1
```
Answer: 2394

2741 × 6 becomes

```
      2  7  4  1
  ×            6
  _____
  1   6  4  4  6
      4  2
```
Answer: 16446

Long multiplication

24 × 16 becomes

```
        2
        2  4
  ×     1  6
  _____
     2  4  0
     1  4  4
  _____
     3  8  4
```
Answer: 384

124 × 26 becomes

```
     1  2
     1  2  4
  ×     2  6
  _____
  2  4  8  0
     7  4  4
  _____
  3  2  2  4
     1  1
```
Answer: 3224

124 × 26 becomes

```
     1  2
     1  2  4
  ×     2  6
  _____
     7  4  4
  2  4  8  0
  _____
  3  2  2  4
     1  1
```
Answer: 3224

Short division

98 ÷ 7 becomes

```
      1   4
  7 | 9  ²8
```

Answer: 14

432 ÷ 5 becomes

```
        8   6   r2
  5 | 4  3³  2
```

Answer: 86 remainder 2

496 ÷ 11 becomes

```
          4   5   r1
  1  1 | 4  9⁵  6
```

Answer: $45\frac{1}{11}$

Long division

432 ÷ 15 becomes

```
          2   8   r12
  1  5 | 4  3   2
         3  0   0
         1  3   2
         1  2   0
            1   2
```

Answer: 28 remainder 12

432 ÷ 15 becomes

```
          2   8
  1  5 | 4  3   2
         3  0   0    15 × 20
         1  3   2
         1  2   0    15 × 8
            1   2
```

$$\frac{12}{15} = \frac{4}{5}$$

Answer: $28\frac{4}{5}$

432 ÷ 15 becomes

```
          2   8  ·  8
  1  5 | 4  3   2  ·  0
         3  0
         1  3   2
         1  2   0
            1   2  ·  0
            1   2  ·  0
                     0
```

Answer: 28.8

WHAT'S NEW
IN THE 2014 CURRICULUM?

- Curriculum aims for children to become develop scientific knowledge and conceptual understanding through the specific disciplines of biology, chemistry and physics, develop understanding of the nature, processes and methods of science and to understand the uses and implications of science, today and for the future
- Year-by-year approach to the Curriculum
- Scientific enquiry has been embedded in the curriculum and renamed 'Working scientifically'
- Stretching curriculum with additional content in Key Stage 2, e.g. Evolution

Scholastic resources that support the 2014 Science Curriculum

100 Science Lessons

100 Science Lessons for the 2014 Curriculum brings you a whole year of inspirational, ready-made lessons fully matched to the new curriculum.

- A whole year planned and ready to teach
- Time-saving pick-up-and-use format
- A trusted series: over a million copies sold
- Every lesson is carefully matched to the new objectives

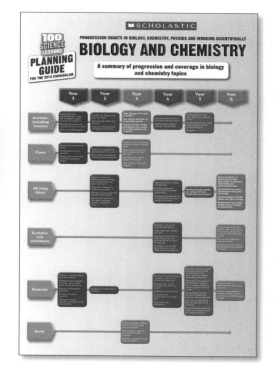

SCHOLASTIC

Investigate

Investigate

Fire imagination and build non-fiction reading skills with this series of high-interest, visually stunning books based around exciting science themes

- Smooth the transition from guided reading to confident independent reading
- Matched to the broad themes of the new science Curriculum (e.g. Light, Sound, Life Cycles)
- Easy to read text combined with dramatic visuals and attention grabbing facts

Scholastic Primary Science

Turn all your students into little scientists with this exciting new science programme from Scholastic. Scholastic Primary Science is a rich and comprehensive resource which covers 120 topics across 4 strands for years 1 to 6.

5 lesson cards
(6 copies of each)

Activities CD-ROM

Order online at www.scholastic.co.uk/education or phone 0845 603 9091.

Science

Purpose of study

A high-quality science education provides the foundations for understanding the world through the specific disciplines of biology, chemistry and physics. Science has changed our lives and is vital to the world's future prosperity, and all pupils should be taught essential aspects of the knowledge, methods, processes and uses of science. Through building up a body of key foundational knowledge and concepts, pupils should be encouraged to recognise the power of rational explanation and develop a sense of excitement and curiosity about natural phenomena. They should be encouraged to understand how science can be used to explain what is occurring, predict how things will behave, and analyse causes.

Aims

The National Curriculum for science aims to ensure that all pupils:

- develop **scientific knowledge and conceptual understanding** through the specific disciplines of biology, chemistry and physics
- develop understanding of the **nature, processes and methods of science** through different types of science enquiries that help them to answer scientific questions about the world around them
- are equipped with the scientific knowledge required to understand the **uses and implications** of science, today and for the future.

Scientific knowledge and conceptual understanding

The Programmes of Study describe a sequence of knowledge and concepts. While it is important that pupils make progress, it is also vitally important that they develop secure understanding of each key block of knowledge and concepts in order to progress to the next stage. Insecure, superficial understanding will not allow genuine progression: pupils may struggle at key points of transition (such as between primary and secondary school), build up serious misconceptions, and/or have significant difficulties in understanding higher-order content.

Pupils should be able to describe associated processes and key characteristics in common language, but they should also be familiar with, and use, technical terminology accurately and precisely. They should build up an extended specialist vocabulary. They should also apply their mathematical knowledge to their understanding of science, including collecting, presenting and analysing data. The social and economic implications of science are important but, generally, they are taught most appropriately within the wider school curriculum: teachers will wish to use different contexts to maximise their pupils' engagement with and motivation to study science.

The nature, processes and methods of science

'Working scientifically' specifies the understanding of the nature, processes and methods of science for each year group. It should not be taught as a separate strand. The notes and guidance give examples of how 'working scientifically' might be embedded within the content of biology, chemistry and physics, focusing on the key features of scientific enquiry, so that pupils learn to use a variety of approaches to answer relevant scientific questions. These types of scientific enquiry should include: observing over time; pattern seeking; identifying, classifying and grouping; comparative and fair testing (controlled investigations); and researching using secondary sources. Pupils should seek answers to questions through collecting, analysing and presenting data. 'Working scientifically' will be developed further at Key Stages 3 and 4, once pupils have built up sufficient understanding of science to engage meaningfully in more sophisticated discussion of experimental design and control.

Spoken language

The National Curriculum for science reflects the importance of spoken language in pupils' development across the whole curriculum – cognitively, socially and linguistically. The quality and variety of language that pupils hear and speak are key factors in developing their scientific vocabulary and articulating scientific concepts clearly and precisely. They must be assisted in making their thinking clear, both to themselves and others, and teachers should ensure that pupils build secure foundations by using discussion to probe and remedy their misconceptions.

School curriculum

The Programmes of Study for science are set out year-by-year for Key Stages 1 and 2. Schools are, however, only required to teach the relevant Programme of Study by the end of the key stage. Within each key stage, schools therefore have the flexibility to introduce content earlier or later than set out in the Programme of Study. In addition, schools can introduce key stage content during an earlier key stage if appropriate. All schools are also required to set out their school curriculum for science on a year-by-year basis and make this information available online.

Attainment targets

By the end of each key stage, pupils are expected to know, apply and understand the matters, skills and processes specified in the relevant Programme of Study.

Schools are not required by law to teach the example content in grey tint or the content indicated as being non-statutory.

Key Stage 1

The principal focus of science teaching in Key Stage 1 is to enable pupils to experience and observe phenomena, looking more closely at the natural and humanly-constructed world around them. They should be encouraged to be curious and ask questions about what they notice. They should be helped to develop their understanding of scientific ideas by using different types of scientific enquiry to answer their own questions, including observing changes over a period of time, noticing patterns, grouping and classifying things, carrying out simple comparative tests, and finding things out using secondary sources of information. They should begin to use simple scientific language to talk about what they have found out and communicate their ideas to a range of audiences in a variety of ways. Most of the learning about science should be done through the use of first-hand practical experiences, but there should also be some use of appropriate secondary sources, such as books, photographs and videos.

'Working scientifically' is described separately in the Programme of Study, but must **always** be taught through and clearly related to the teaching of substantive science content in the Programme of Study. Throughout the notes and guidance, examples show how scientific methods and skills might be linked to specific elements of the content.

Pupils should read and spell scientific vocabulary at a level consistent with their increasing word reading and spelling knowledge at Key Stage 1.

Working scientifically

Key Stage 1 Programme of Study (statutory requirements)	Notes and guidance (non-statutory)
Working scientifically	**Working scientifically**
During Years 1 and 2, pupils should be taught to use the following practical scientific methods, processes and skills through the teaching of the Programme of Study content: • asking simple questions and recognising that they can be answered in different ways • observing closely, using simple equipment • performing simple tests • identifying and classifying • using their observations and ideas to suggest answers to questions • gathering and recording data to help in answering questions.	Pupils in Years 1 and 2 should explore the world around them and raise their own questions. They should experience different types of scientific enquiries, including practical activities, and begin to recognise ways in which they might answer scientific questions. They should use simple features to compare objects, materials and living things and, with help, decide how to sort and group them, observe changes over time, and, with guidance, they should begin to notice patterns and relationships. They should ask people questions and use simple secondary sources to find answers. They should use simple measurements and equipment (eg hand lenses, egg timers) to gather data, carry out simple tests, record simple data, and talk about what they have found out and how they found it out. With help, they should record and communicate their findings in a range of ways and begin to use simple scientific language. These opportunities for working scientifically should be provided across Years 1 and 2 so that the expectations in the Programme of Study can be met by the end of Year 2. Pupils are not expected to cover each aspect for every area of study.
Plants	**Plants**
Pupils should be taught to: • identify and name a variety of common wild and garden plants, including deciduous and evergreen trees • identify and describe the basic structure of a variety of common flowering plants, including trees.	Pupils should use the local environment throughout the year to explore and answer questions about plants growing in their habitat. Where possible, they should observe the growth of flowers and vegetables that they have planted. They should become familiar with common names of flowers, examples of deciduous and evergreen trees, and plant structures (including leaves flowers (blossom), petals, fruit, roots, buld, seed, trunk, branches, stem).

Year 1

Year 1 Programme of Study (statutory requirements)	Notes and guidance (non-statutory)
	Pupils might work scientifically by: observing closely, perhaps using magnifying glasses, and comparing and contrasting familiar plants; describing how they were able to identify and group them, and drawing diagrams showing the parts of different plants including trees. Pupils might keep records of how plants have changed over time, for example the leaves falling off trees and buds opening; and compare and contrast what they have found out about different plants.
Animals, including humans Pupils should be taught to: • identify and name a variety of common animals, including fish, amphibians, reptiles, birds and mammals • identify and name a variety of common animals that are carnivores, herbivores and omnivores • describe and compare the structure of a variety of common animals (fish, amphibians, reptiles, birds and mammals including pets) • identify, name, draw and label the basic parts of the human body and say which part of the body is associated with each sense.	**Animals, including humans** Pupils should use the local environment throughout the year to explore and answer questions about animals in their habitat. They should understand how to take care of animals taken from their local environment and the need to return them safely after study. Pupils should become familiar with the common names of some fish, amphibians, reptiles birds and mammals, including those that are kept as pets. Pupils should have plenty of opportunities to learn the names of the main body parts (including head, neck, arms, elbows, legs, knees, face, ears, eyes, hair, mouth, teeth) through games, actions, songs and rhymes. Pupils might work scientifically by: using their observations to compare and contrast animals at first hand or through videos and photographs, describing how they identify and group them; grouping animals according to what they eat; and using their senses to compare different textures, sounds and smells.

Year 1 Programme of Study (statutory requirements)	Notes and guidance (non-statutory)
Everyday materials Pupils should be taught to: • distinguish between an object and the material from which it is made • identify and name a variety of everyday materials, including wood, plastic, glass, metal, water and rock • describe the simple physical properties of a variety of everyday materials • compare	**Everyday materials** Pupils should explore, name, discuss and raise and answer questions about everyday materials so that they become familiar with the names of materials and properties such as: hard/soft; stretchy/stiff; shiny/dull; rough/smooth; bendy/not bendy; waterproof/not waterproof; absorbent/not absorbent; opaque/transparent. Pupils should explore and experiment with a wide variety of materials, not only those listed in the Programme of Study, but including for example: brick, paper, fabrics, elastic, foil.
• compare and group together a variety of everyday materials on the basis of their simple physical properties	Pupils might work scientifically by: performing simple tests to explore questions, for example, 'What is the best material for an umbrella? … for lining a dog basket? … for curtains? … for a bookshelf? … for a gymnast's leotard?'
Seasonal changes Pupils should be taught to: • observe changes across the four seasons • observe and describe weather associated with the seasons and how day length varies.	**Seasonal changes** Pupils should observe and talk about changes in the weather and the seasons. **Note:** Pupils should be warned that it is not safe to look directly at the Sun, even when wearing dark glasses. Pupils might work scientifically by: making tables and charts about the weather; and making displays of what happens in the world around them, including day length, as the seasons change.

Year 2

Year 2 Programme of Study (statutory requirements)	Notes and guidance (non-statutory)
Living things and their habitats	**Living things and their habitats**
Pupils should be taught to:	Pupils should be introduced to the idea that all living things have certain characteristics that are essential for keeping them alive and healthy. They should raise and answer questions that help them to become familiar with the life processes that are common to all living things. Pupils should be introduced to the terms 'habitat' (a natural environment or home of a variety of plants and animals) and 'micro-habitat' (a very small habitat, for woodlice under stones, logs or leaf litter, for example). They should raise and answer questions about the local environment that help them to identify and study a variety of plants and animals within their habitat and observe how living things depend on each other, for example plants serving as a source of food and shelter for animals. Pupils should compare animals in familiar habitats with animals found in less familiar habitats, for example, on the seashore, in woodland, in the ocean, in the rainforest.
• explore and compare the differences between things that are living, dead, and things that have never been alive	
• identify that most living things live in habitats to which they are suited and describe how different habitats provide for the basic needs of different kinds of animals and plants, and how they depend on each other	
• identify and name a variety of plants and animals in their habitats, including micro-habitats	Pupils might work scientifically by: sorting and classifying things according to whether they are living, dead or were never alive, and recording their findings using charts. They should describe how they decided where to place things, exploring questions such as: 'Is a flame alive?' 'Is a deciduous tree dead in winter?' and talk about ways of answering their questions. They could construct a simple food chain that includes humans (e.g. grass, cow, human). They could describe the conditions in different habitats and micro-habitats (under log, on stony path, under bushes) and find out how the conditions affect the number and type(s) of plants and animals that live there.
• describe how animals obtain their food from plants and other animals, using the idea of a simple food chain, and identify and name different sources of food.	

■■SCHOLASTIC

Year 2 Programme of Study (statutory requirements)	Notes and guidance (non-statutory)
Plants Pupils should be taught to: • observe and describe how seeds and bulbs grow into mature plants • find out and describe how plants need water, light and a suitable temperature to grow and stay healthy.	**Plants** Pupils should use the local environment throughout the year to observe how different plants grow. Pupils should be introduced to the requirements of plants for germination, growth and survival, as well as to the processes of reproduction and growth in plants. **Note:** Seeds and bulbs need water to grow but most do not need light; seeds and bulbs have a store of food inside them. Pupils might work scientifically by: observing and recording, with some accuracy, the growth of a variety of plants as they change over time from a seed or bulb, or observing similar plants at different stages of growth; setting up a comparative test to show that plants need light and water to stay healthy.
Animals, including humans Pupils should be taught to: • notice that animals, including humans, have offspring which grow into adults • find out about and describe the basic needs of animals, including humans, for survival (water, food and air) • describe the importance for humans of exercise, eating the right amounts of different types of food, and hygiene.	**Animals, including humans** Pupils should be introduced to the basic needs of animals for survival, as well as the importance of exercise and nutrition for humans. They should also be introduced to the processes of reproduction and growth in animals. The focus at this stage should be on questions that help pupils to recognise growth; they should not be expected to understand how reproduction occurs. The following examples might be used: egg, chick, chicken; egg, caterpillar, pupa, butterfly; spawn, tadpole, frog; lamb, sheep. Growing into adults can include reference to baby, toddler, child, teenager, adult. Pupils might work scientifically by: observing through video or first-hand observation and measurement how different animals, including humans, grow; asking questions about what things animals need for survival and what humans need to stay healthy; and suggesting ways to find answers to their questions.

Year 2 Programme of Study (statutory requirements)	Notes and guidance (non-statutory)
Uses of everyday materials Pupils should be taught to: • identify and compare the uses of a variety of everyday materials, including wood, metal, plastic, glass, brick, rock, paper and cardboard for particular uses • find out how the shapes of solid objects made from some materials can be changed by squashing, bending, twisting and stretching	**Uses of everyday materials** Pupils should identify and discuss the uses of different everyday materials so that they become familiar with how some materials are used for more than one thing (metal can be used for coins, cans, cars and table legs; wood can be used for matches, floors, and telegraph poles) or different materials are used for the same thing (spoons can be made from plastic, wood, metal, but not normally from glass). They should think about the properties of materials that make them suitable or unsuitable for particular purposes and they should be encouraged to think about unusual and creative uses for everyday materials. Pupils might find out about people who have developed useful new materials, for example John Dunlop, Charles Macintosh or John McAdam. Pupils might work scientifically by: comparing the uses of everyday materials in and around the school with materials found in other places (at home, on the journey to school, on visits, and in stories, rhymes and songs); observing closely, identifying and classifying the uses of different materials, and recording their observations.

Lower Key Stage 2 – Years 3–4

The principal focus of science teaching in lower Key Stage 2 is to enable pupils to broaden their scientific view of the world around them. They should do this through exploring, talking about, testing and developing ideas about everyday phenomena and the relationships between living things and familiar environments, and by beginning to develop their ideas about functions, relationships and interactions. They should ask their own questions about what they observe and make some decisions about which types of scientific enquiry are likely to be the best ways of answering them, including observing changes over time, noticing patterns, grouping and classifying things, carrying out simple comparative and fair tests and finding things out using secondary sources of information. They should draw simple conclusions and use some scientific language, first, to talk about and, later, to write about what they have found out.

'Working scientifically' is described separately at the beginning of the Programme of Study, but must **always** be taught through and clearly related to substantive science content in the Programme of Study. Throughout the notes and guidance, examples show how scientific methods and skills might be linked to specific elements of the content.

Pupils should read and spell scientific vocabulary correctly and with confidence, using their growing word reading and spelling knowledge.

Working scientifically

Lower Key Stage 2 Programme of Study (statutory requirements)	Notes and guidance (non-statutory)
Working scientifically During Years 3 and 4, pupils should be taught to use the following practical scientific methods, processes and skills through the teaching of the Programme of Study content: • asking relevant questions and using different types of scientific enquiries to answer them • setting up simple practical enquiries, comparative and fair tests • making systematic and careful observations and, where appropriate, taking accurate measurements using standard units, using a range of equipment, including thermometers and data loggers • gathering, recording, classifying and presenting data in a variety of ways to help in answering questions • recording findings using simple scientific language, drawings, labelled diagrams, keys, bar charts and tables • reporting on findings from enquiries, including oral and written explanations, displays or presentations of results and conclusions • using results to draw simple conclusions, make predictions for new values, suggest improvements and raise further questions • identifying differences, similarities or changes related to simple scientific ideas and processes • using straightforward scientific evidence to answer questions or to support their findings.	**Working scientifically** Pupils in Years 3 and 4 should be given a range of scientific experiences to enable them to raise their own questions about the world around them. They should start to make their own decisions about the most appropriate type of scientific enquiry they might use to answer questions; recognise when a simple fair test is necessary and help to decide how to set it up; talk about criteria for grouping, sorting and classifying; and use simple keys. They should begin to look for naturally occurring patterns and relationships and decide what data to collect to identify them. They should help to make decisions about what observations to make, how long to make them for and the type of simple equipment that might be used. They should learn how to use new equipment, such as data loggers, appropriately. They should collect data from their own observations and measurements, using notes, simple tables and standard units, and help to make decisions about how to record and analyse this data. With help, pupils should look for changes, patterns, similarities and differences in their data in order to draw simple conclusions and answer questions. With support, they should identify new questions arising from the data, making predictions for new values within or beyond the data they have collected and finding ways of improving what they have already done. They should also recognise when and how secondary sources might help them to answer questions that cannot be answered through practical investigations. Pupils should use relevant scientific language to discuss their ideas and communicate their findings in ways that are appropriate for different audiences. These opportunities for working scientifically should be provided across Years 3 and 4 so that the expectations in the Programme of Study can be met by the end of Year 4. Pupils are not expected to cover each aspect for every area of study.

Year 3

Year 3 Programme of Study (statutory requirements)	Notes and guidance (non-statutory)
Plants Pupils should be taught to: • identify and describe the functions of different parts of flowering plants: roots, stem/trunk, leaves and flowers • explore the requirements of plants for life and growth (air, light, water, nutrients from soil, and room to grow) and how they vary from plant to plant • investigate the way in which water is transported within plants • explore the part that flowers play in the life cycle of flowering plants, including pollination, seed formation and seed dispersal.	**Plants** Pupils should be introduced to the relationship between structure and function: the idea that every part has a job to do. They should explore questions that focus on the role of the roots and stem in nutrition and support, leaves for nutrition and flowers for reproduction. **Note:** Pupils can be introduced to the idea that plants can make their own food, but at this stage they do not need to understand how this happens. Pupils might work scientifically by: comparing the effect of different factors on plant growth, for example the amount of light, the amount of fertiliser; discovering how seeds are formed by observing the different stages of plant life cycles over a period of time; looking for patterns in the structure of fruits that relate to how the seeds are dispersed. They might observe how water is transported in plants, for example by putting cut, white carnations into coloured water and observing how water travels up the stem to the flowers.
Animals, including humans Pupils should be taught to: • identify that animals, including humans, need the right types and amount of nutrition, and that they cannot make their own food; they get nutrition from what they eat • identify that humans and some animals have skeletons and muscles for support, protection and movement.	**Animals, including humans** Pupils should continue to learn about the importance of nutrition and should be introduced to the main body parts associated with the skeleton and muscles, finding out how different parts of the body have special functions. Pupils might work scientifically by: identifying and grouping animals with and without skeletons and observing and comparing their movement; exploring ideas about what would happen if humans did not have skeletons. They might compare and contrast the diets of different animals (including their pets) and decide ways of grouping them according to what they eat. They might research different food groups and how they keep us healthy and design meals based on what they find out.

Year 3 Programme of Study (statutory requirements)	Notes and guidance (non-statutory)
Rocks Pupils should be taught to: • compare and group together different kinds of rocks on the basis of their appearance and simple physical properties • describe in simple terms how fossils are formed when things that have lived are trapped within rock • recognise that soils are made from rocks and organic matter.	**Rocks** Linked with work in geography, pupils should explore different kinds of rocks and soils, including those in the local environment. Pupils might work scientifically by: observing rocks, including those used in buildings and gravestones, and exploring how and why they might have changed over time; using a hand lens or microscope to help them to identify and classify rocks according to whether they have grains or crystals, and whether they have fossils in them. Pupils might research and discuss the different kinds of living things whose fossils are found in sedimentary rock and explore how fossils are formed. Pupils could explore different soils and identify similarities and differences between them and investigate what happens when rocks are rubbed together or what changes occur when they are in water. They can raise and answer questions about the way soils are formed.
Light Pupils should be taught to: • recognise that they need light in order to see things and that dark is the absence of light • notice that light is reflected from surfaces • recognise that light from the sun can be dangerous and that there are ways to protect their eyes • recognise that shadows are formed when the light from a light source is blocked by a solid object • find patterns in the way that the size of shadows change	**Light** Pupils should explore what happens when light reflects off a mirror or other reflective surfaces, including playing mirror games to help them to answer questions about how light behaves. They should think about why it is important to protect their eyes from bright lights. They should look for, and measure, shadows, and find out how they are formed and what might cause the shadows to change. **Note:** Pupils should be warned that it is not safe to look directly at the Sun, even when wearing dark glasses. Pupils might work scientifically by: looking for patterns in what happens to shadows when the light source moves or the distance between the light source and the object changes.

Year 3 Programme of Study (statutory requirements)

Forces and magnets

Pupils should be taught to:

- compare how things ove on different surfaces

- notice that some forces need contact between two objects, but magnetic forces can act at a distance

- observe how magnets attract or repel each other and attract some materials and not others

- compare and group together a variety of everyday materials on the basis of whether they are attracted to a magnet, and identify some magnetic materials

- describe magnets as having two poles

- predict whether two magnets will attract or repel each other, depending on which poles are facing.

Notes and guidance (non-statutory)

Forces and magnets

Pupils should observe that magnetic forces can act without direct contact, unlike most forces, where direct contact is necessary (for example, opening a door, pushing a swing). They should explore the behaviour and everyday uses of different magnets (for example, bar, ring, button and horseshoe).

Pupils might work scientifically by: comparing how different things move and grouping them; raising questions and carrying out tests to find out how far things move on different surfaces and gathering and recording data to find answers to their questions; exploring the strengths of different magnets and finding a fair way to compare them; sorting materials into those that are magnetic and those that are not; looking for patterns in the way that magnets behave in relation to each other and what might affect this, such as the strength of the magnet or which pole faces another; identifying how these properties make magnets useful in everyday items and suggesting creative uses for different magnets.

Year 4

Year 4 Programme of Study (statutory requirements)	Notes and guidance (non-statutory)
Living things and their habitats Pupils should be taught to: • recognise that living things can be grouped in a variety of ways • explore and use classification keys to help group, identify and name a variety of living things in their local and wider environment • recognise that environments can change and that this can sometimes pose dangers to living things	**Living things and their habitats** Pupils should use the local environment throughout the year to raise and answer questions that help them to identify and study plants and animals in their habitat. They should identify how the habitat changes throughout the year. Pupils should explore possible ways of grouping a wide selection of living things that include animals and flowering plants and non-flowering plants. Pupils could begin to put vertebrate animals into groups such as fish, amphibians, reptiles, birds, and mammals; and invertebrates into snails and slugs, worms, spiders and insects. **Note:** Plants can be grouped into categories such as flowering plants (including grasses) and non-flowering plants, such as ferns and mosses. Pupils should explore examples of human impact (both positive and negative) on environments, such as the positive effects of nature reserves, ecologically planned parks, or garden ponds, and the negative effects of population and development, litter or deforestation. Pupils might work scientifically by: using and making simple guides or keys to explore and identify local plants and animals; making a guide to local living things; raising and answering questions based on their observations of animals and what they have found out about other animals that they have researched.
Animals, including humans Pupils should be taught to: • describe the simple functions of the basic parts of the digestive system in humans • identify the different types of teeth in humans and their simple functions • construct and interpret a variety of food chains, identifying producers, predators and prey.	**Animals, including humans** Pupils should be introduced to the main body parts associated with the digestive system, such as mouth, tongue, teeth, oesophagus, stomach and intestine and explore questions that help them to understand their special functions. Pupils might work scientifically by: comparing the teeth of carnivores and herbivores, and suggesting reasons for differences; finding out what damages teeth and how to look after them. They might draw and discuss their ideas about the digestive system and compare them with models or images.

Year 4 Programme of Study (statutory requirements)	Notes and guidance (non-statutory)
States of matter	**States of matter**
Pupils should be taught to:	Pupils should explore a variety of everyday materials and develop simple descriptions of the states of matter (solids hold their shape; liquids form a pool not a pile; gases escape from an unsealed container). Pupils should observe water as a solid, a liquid and a gas and should note the changes to water when it is heated or cooled.
• compare and group materials together, according to whether they are solids, liquids or gases	
• observe that some materials change state when they are heated or cooled, and measure or research the temperature at which this happens in degrees Celsius (°C)	**Note:** Teachers should avoid using materials where heating is associated with chemical change, for example, through baking or burning.
• identify the part played by evaporation and condensation in the water cycle and associate the rate of evaporation with temperature.	Pupils might work scientifically by: grouping and classifying a variety of different materials; exploring the effect of temperature on substances such as chocolate, butter, cream (for example, to make food such as chocolate crispy cakes and ice cream for a party). They could research the temperature at which materials change state, such as when iron melts or when oxygen condenses into a liquid. They might observe and record evaporation over a period of time, such as a puddle in the playground or washing on a line, and investigate the effect of temperature on washing drying or snowmen melting.
Sound	**Sound**
Pupils should be taught to:	Pupils should explore and identify the way sound is made through vibration in a range of different musical instruments from around the world; and find out how the pitch and volume of sounds can be changed in a variety of ways.
• identify how sounds are made, associating some of them with something vibrating	
• recognise that vibrations from sounds travel through a medium to the ear	Pupils might work scientifically by: finding patterns in the sounds that are made by different ojects such as saucepan lids of different sizes or elastic bands of different thicknesses. They might make earmuffs from a variety of different materials to investigate which provides the best insulation against sound. They could make and play their own instruments by using what they have found out about pitch and volume.
• find patterns between the pitch of a sound and features of the object that produced it	
• find patterns between the volume of a sound and the strength of the vibrations that produced it	
• recognise that sounds get fainter as the distance from the sound source increases	

Year 4 Programme of Study (statutory requirements)	Notes and guidance (non-statutory)
Electricity	**Electricity**
Pupils should be taught to:	Pupils should construct simple series circuits, trying different components, such as bulbs, buzzers and motors, and including switches, and use their circuits to create simple devices. Pupils should draw the circuit as a pictorial representation, not necessarily using conventional circuit symbols at this stage; these will be introduced in Year 6.
• identify common appliances that run on electricity	
• construct a simple series electrical circuit, identifying and naming its basic parts, including cells, wires, bulbs, switches and buzzers	
• identify whether or not a lamp will light in a simple series circuit, based on whether or not the lamp is part of a complete loop with a battery	**Note:** Pupils might use the terms current and voltage, but these should not be introduced or defined formally at this stage. Pupils should be taught about precautions for working safely with electricity.
• recognise that a switch opens and closes a circuit and associate this with whether or not a lamp lights in a simple series circuit	Pupils might work scientifically by: observing patterns, for example that bulbs get brighter if more cells are added, that metals tend to be conductors of electricity, and that some materials can and some cannot be used to connect across a gap in a circuit.
• recognise some common conductors and insulators, and associate metals with being good conductors.	

Upper Key Stage 2 – Years 5–6

The principal focus of science teaching in upper Key Stage 2 is to enable pupils to develop a deeper understanding of a wide range of scientific ideas. They should do this through exploring and talking about their ideas; asking their own questions about scientific phenomena; and analysing functions, relationships and interactions more systematically. At upper Key Stage 2, they should encounter more abstract ideas and begin to recognise how these ideas help them to understand and predict how the world operates. They should also begin to recognise that scientific ideas change and develop over time. They should select the most appropriate ways to answer science questions using different types of scientific enquiry, including observing changes over different periods of time, noticing patterns, grouping and classifying things, carrying out comparative and fair tests and finding things out using a wide range of secondary sources of information. Pupils should draw conclusions based on their data and observations, use evidence to justify their ideas, and use their scientific knowledge and understanding to explain their findings.

'Working and thinking scientifically' is described separately at the beginning of the Programme of Study, but must **always** be taught through and clearly related to substantive science content in the Programme of Study. Throughout the notes and guidance, examples show how scientific methods and skills might be linked to specific elements of the content.

Pupils should read, spell and pronounce scientific vocabulary correctly.

Working scientifically

Upper Key Stage 2 Programme of Study (statutory requirements)	Notes and guidance (non-statutory)
Working scientifically	**Working scientifically**
During Years 5 and 6, pupils should be taught to use the following practical scientific methods, processes and skills through the teaching of the Programme of Study content: • planning different types of scientific enquiries to answer questions, including recognising and controlling variables where necessary • taking measurements, using a range of scientific equipment, with increasing accuracy and precision, taking repeat readings where appropriate • recording data and results of increasing complexity using scientific diagrams and labels, classification keys, tables, and bar and line graphs • using test results to make predictions to set up further comparative and fair tests • reporting and presenting findings from enquiries, including conclusions, causal relationships and explanations of results, in oral and written forms such as displays and other presentations • identifying scientific evidence that has been used to support or refute ideas or arguments.	Pupils in Years 5 and 6 should use their science experiences to: explore ideas and raise different kinds of questions; select and plan the most appropriate type of scientific enquiry to use to answer scientific questions; recognise when and how to set up comparative and fair tests and explain which variables need to be controlled and why. They should use and develop keys and other information records to identify, classify and describe living things and materials, and identify patterns that might be found in the natural environment. They should make their own decisions about what observations to make, what measurements to use and how long to make them for, and whether to repeat them; choose the most appropriate equipment to make measurements and explain how to use it accurately. They should decide how to record data from a choice of familiar approaches; look for different causal relationships in their data and identify evidence that refutes or supports their ideas. They should use their results to identify when further tests and observations might be needed; recognise which secondary sources will be most useful to research their ideas and begin to separate opinion from fact. They should use relevant scientific language and illustrations to discuss, communicate and justify their scientific ideas and should talk about how scientific ideas have developed over time. These opportunities for working scientifically should be provided across Years 5 and 6 so that the expectations in the Programme of Study can be met by the end of Year 6. Pupils are not expected to cover each aspect for every area of study.

Year 5

Year 5 Programme of Study (statutory requirements)	Notes and guidance (non-statutory)
All living things and their habitats Pupils should be taught to: • describe the differences in the life cycles of a mammal, an amphibian, an insect and a bird • describe the life process of reproduction in some plants and animals.	**All living things and their habitats** Pupils should study and raise questions about their local environment throughout the year. They should observe life-cycle changes in a variety of living things, for example plants in the vegetable garden or flower border, and animals in the local environment. They should find out about the work of naturalists and animal behaviourists, for example, David Attenborough and Jane Goodall. Pupils should find out about different types of reproduction, including sexual and asexual reproduction in plants, and sexual reproduction in animals. Pupils might work scientifically by: observing and comparing the life cycles of plants and animals in their local environment with other plants and animals around the world (in the rainforest, in the oceans, in desert areas and in prehistoric times), asking pertinent questions and suggesting reasons for similarities and differences. They might try to grow new plants from different parts of the parent plant, for example seeds, stem and root cuttings, tubers, bulbs. They might observe changes in an animal over a period of time (for example, by hatching and rearing chicks), comparing how different animals reproduce and grow.
Animals, including humans Pupils should be taught to: • describe the changes as humans develop to old age.	**Animals, including humans** Pupils should draw a timeline to indicate stages in the growth and development of humans. They should learn about the changes experienced in puberty. Pupils could work scientifically by researching the gestation periods of other animals and comparing them with humans; by finding out and recording the length and mass of a baby as it grows.

Year 5 Programme of Study (statutory requirements)

Properties and changes of materials

Pupils should be taught to:

- compare and group together everyday materials on the basis of their properties, including their hardness, solubility, transparency, conductivity (electrical and thermal), and response to magnets

- know that some materials will dissolve in liquid to form a solution, and describe how to recover a substance from a solution

- use knowledge of solids, liquids and gases to decide how mixtures might be separated, including through filtering, sieving and evaporating

- give reasons, based on evidence from comparative and fair tests, for the particular uses of everyday materials, including metals, wood and plastic

- demonstrate that dissolving, mixing and changes of state are reversible changes

- explain that some changes result in the formation of new materials, and that this kind of change is not usually reversible, including changes associated with burning and the action of acid on bicarbonate of soda

Notes and guidance (non-statutory)

Properties and changes of materials

Pupils should build a more systematic understanding of materials by exploring and comparing the properties of a broad range of materials, including relating these to what they learned about magnetism in Year 3 and about electricity in Year 4. They should explore reversible changes, including evaporating, filtering, sieving, melting and dissolving, recognising that melting and dissolving are different processes. Pupils should explore changes that are difficult to reverse, such as burning, rusting and other reactions, for example vinegar with bicarbonate of soda. They should find out about how chemists create new materials, for example Spencer Silver, who invented the glue for sticky notes or Ruth Benerito, who invented wrinkle-free cotton.

Note: Pupils are not required to make quantitative measurements about conductivity and insulation at this stage. It is sufficient for them to observe that some conductors will produce a brighter bulb in a circuit than others and that some materials will feel hotter than others when a heat source is placed against them. Safety guidelines should be followed when burning materials.

Pupils might work scientifically by: carrying out tests to answer questions such as 'Which materials would be the most effective for making a warm jacket, for wrapping ice cream to stop it melting, or for making blackout curtains?' They might compare materials in order to make a switch in a circuit. They could observe and compare the changes that take place, for example when burning different materials or baking bread or cakes. They might research and discuss how chemical changes have an impact on our lives, for example cooking, and discuss the creative use of new materials such as polymers, super-sticky and super-thin materials.

Year 5 Programme of Study (statutory requirements)

Earth and space

Pupils should be taught to:

- describe the movement of the Earth, and other planets, relative to the Sun in the solar system

- describe the movement of the Moon relative to the Earth

- describe the Sun, Earth and Moon as approximately spherical bodies

- use the idea of the Earth's rotation to explain day and night and the apparent movement of the sun across the sky

Notes and guidance (non-statutory)

Earth and space

Pupils should be introduced to a model of the Sun and Earth that enables them to explain day and night. Pupils should learn that the Sun is a star at the centre of our solar system and that it has eight planets: Mercury, Venus, Earth, Mars, Jupiter, Saturn, Uranus and Neptune (Pluto was reclassified as a 'dwarf planet' in 2006). They should understand that a moon is a celestial body that orbits a planet (Earth has one moon; Jupiter has four large moons and numerous smaller ones).

Note: Pupils should be warned that it is not safe to look directly at the Sun, even when wearing dark glasses.

Pupils should find out about the way that ideas about the solar system have developed, understanding how the geocentric model of the solar system gave way to the heliocentric model by considering the work of scientists such as Ptolemy, Alhazen and Copernicus.

Pupils might work scientifically by: comparing the time of day at different places on the Earth through Internet links and direct communication; creating simple models of the solar system; constructing simple shadow clocks and sundials, calibrated to show midday and the start and end of the school day; finding out why some people think that structures such as Stonehenge might have been used as astronomical clocks.

SCHOLASTIC

Year 5 Programme of Study (statutory requirements)	Notes and guidance (non-statutory)
Forces Pupils should be taught to: • explain that unsupported objects fall towards the Earth because of the force of gravity acting between the Earth and the falling object • identify the effects of air resistance, water resistance and friction, that act between moving surfaces • recognise that some mechanisms, including levers, pulleys and gears, allow a smaller force to have a greater effect	**Forces** Pupils should explore falling objects and raise questions about the effects of air resistance. They should explore the effects of air resistance by observing how different objects such as parachutes and sycamore seeds fall. They should experience forces that make things begin to move, get faster or slow down. Pupils should explore the effects of friction on movement and find out how it slows or stops moving objects, for example by observing the effects of a brake on a bicycle wheel. Pupils should explore the effects of levers, pulleys and simple machines on movement. Pupils might find out how scientists such as Galileo Galilei and Isaac Newton helped to develop the theory of gravitation. Pupils might work scientifically by: exploring falling paper cones or cupcake cases, and designing and making a variety of parachutes and carrying out fair tests to determine which designs are the most effective. They might explore resistance in water by making and testing boats of different shapes. They might design and make artefacts that use simple levers, pulleys, gears and/or springs and explore their effects.

Year 6

Year 6 Programme of Study (statutory requirements)	Notes and guidance (non-statutory)
Living things and their habitats Pupils should be taught to: • describe how living things are classified into broad groups according to common observable characteristics and based on similarities and differences, including micro-organisms, plants and animals • give reasons for classifying plants and animals based on specific characteristics.	**All living things** Pupils should build on their learning about grouping living things in Year 4 by looking at the classification system in more detail. They should be introduced to the idea that broad groupings, such as micro-organisms, plants and animals can be subdivided. Through direct observations where possible, they should classify animals into commonly found invertebrates (eg insects, spiders, snails, worms) and vertebrates (reptiles, fish, amphibians, birds and mammals) and. They should discuss reasons why living things are placed in one group and not another. Pupils might find out about the significance of the work of scientists such as Carl Linnaeus, a pioneer of classification. Pupils might work scientifically by: using classification systems and keys to identify some animals and plants in the immediate environment. They could research unfamiliar animals and plantsfrom a broad range of other habitats and decide where they belong in the classification system.
Animals including humans • identify and name the main parts of the human circulatory system, and describe the functions of the heart, blood vessels and blood • recognise the impact of diet, exercise, drugs and lifestyle on the way their bodies function • describe the ways in which nutrients and water are transported within animals, including humans.	**Animals including humans** Pupils should build on their learning from Years 3 and 4 about the main body parts and internal organs (skeletal, muscular and digestive system) to explore and answer questions that help them to understand how the circulatory system enables the body to function. Pupils should learn how to keep their bodies healthy and how their bodies might be damaged – including how some drugs and other substances can be harmful to the human body. Pupils might work scientifically by: exploring the work of scientists and scientific research about the relationship between diet, exercise, drugs, lifestyle and health.

Year 6 Programme of Study (statutory requirements)	Notes and guidance (non-statutory)
Evolution and inheritance Pupils should be taught to: • recognise that living things have changed over time and that fossils provide information about living things that inhabited the Earth millions of years ago • recognise that living things produce offspring of the same kind, but normally offspring vary and are not identical to their parents • identify how animals and plants are adapted to suit their environment in different ways and that adaptation may lead to evolution.	**Evolution and inheritance** Building on what they learned about fossils in the topic on rocks in Year 3, pupils should find out more about how living things on The Earth have changed over time. They should be introduced to the idea that characteristics are passed from parents to their offspring, for instance by considering different breeds of dogs, and what happens when, for example, labradors are crossed with poodles. They should also appreciate that variation in offspring over time can make animals more or less able to survive in particular environments, for example by exploring how giraffes' necks got longer, or the development of insulating fur on the arctic fox. Pupils might find out about the work of palaeontologists such as Mary Anning and about how Charles Darwin and Alfred Wallace developed their ideas on evolution. **Note:** At this stage, pupils are not expected to understand how genes and chromosomes work. Pupils might work scientifically by: observing and raising questions about local animals and how they are adapted to their environment; comparing how some living things are adapted to survive in extreme conditions, for example cactuses, penguins and camels. They might analyse the advantages and disadvantages of specific adaptations, such as being on two feet rather than four, having a long or a short beak, having gills or lungs, tendrils on climbing plants, brightly coloured and scented flowers.

Year 6 Programme of Study (statutory requirements)	Notes and guidance (non-statutory)
Light Pupils should be taught to: • recognise that light appears to travel in straight lines • use the idea that light travels in straight lines to explain that objects are seen because they give out or reflect light into the eye • explain that we see things because light travels from light sources to our eyes or from light sources to objects and then to our eyes • use the idea that light travels in straight lines to explain why shadows have the same shape as the objects that cast them.	**Light** Pupils should build on light in year 3, exploring the way that light behaves, including light sources, reflection and shadows. They should talk about what happens and make predictions. Pupils might work scientifically by: deciding where to place rearview mirrors on cars; designing and making a periscope and using the idea that light appears to travel in straight lines to explain how it works. They might investigate the relationship between light sources, objects and shadows by using shadow puppets. They could extend their experience of light by looking at a arange of phenomena including rainbows, colours on soap bubbles, objects looking bent in water and coloured filters (they do not need to explain why these phenomena occur)
Electricity Pupils should be taught to: • associate the brightness of a lamp or the volume of a buzzer with the number and voltage of cells used in the circuit • compare and give reasons for variations in how components function, including the brightness of bulbs, the loudness of buzzers and the on/off position of switches • use recognised symbols when representing a simple circuit in a diagram.	**Electricity** Building on their work in Year 4, pupils should construct simple series circuits, to help them to answer questions about what happens when they try different components, for example, switches, bulbs, buzzers and motors. They should learn how to represent a simple circuit in a diagram using recognised symbols. **Note:** Pupils are expected to learn only about series circuits, not parallel circuits. Pupils should be taught to take the necessary precautions for working safely with electricity. Pupils might work scientifically by: systematically identifying the effect of changing one component at a time in a circuit; designing and making a set of traffic lights, a burglar alarm or some other useful circuit.

WHAT'S NEW
IN THE 2014 CURRICULUM?

- New Languages Curriculum at Key Stage 2 (see pages 151-152)
- New requirement to teach History chronologically; focus on study up to 1066 at primary school (see pages 147-150)
- Increased expectations of skills development in Geography, especially map work (see pages 144-146)
- New Computing Curriculum places much greater emphasis on teaching the principles of computational thinking and practical programming skills (see pages 139-140)

Scholastic resources that support the 2014 English Curriculum

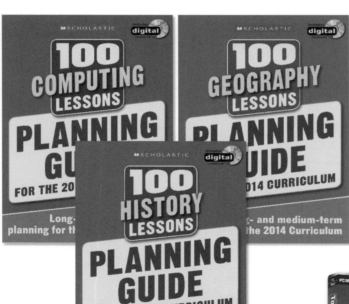

100 History, 100 Computing, 100 Geography

100 History Lesson, 100 Geography Lessons and 100 Computing Lessons bring you all of the planning and teaching you will need to deliver the new curriculum in these subjects. They provide a whole year of inspirational, ready-made lessons fully matched to the 2014 Curriculum.

- Master the new curriculum: every lesson is carefully matched to the new objectives
- A whole year planned and ready to teach
- Time-saving pick-up-and-use format
- A trusted series: over a million copies sold

Hot Topics

Inspire children's creativity through these favourite topics linked closely to the new Curriculum.

- Three levels of activity provide ready made opportunities for work across the school
- Banks of images and videos enable rich presentations to support each topic
- National Curriculum grids are provided in editable Word format to allow teachers to integrate each theme into their own planning

Order online at www.scholastic.co.uk/education or phone 0845 603 9091.

■ SCHOLASTIC

Art and design

Purpose of study

Art, craft and design embody some of the highest forms of human creativity. A high-quality art and design education should engage, inspire and challenge pupils, equipping them with the knowledge and skills to experiment, invent and create their own works of art, craft and design. As pupils progress, they should be able to think critically and develop a more rigorous understanding of art and design. They should also know how art and design both reflect and shape our history, and contribute to the culture, creativity and wealth of our nation.

Aims

The National Curriculum for art and design aims to ensure that all pupils:

* produce creative work, exploring their ideas and recording their experiences
* become proficient in drawing, painting, sculpture and other art, craft and design techniques
* evaluate and analyse creative works using the language of art, craft and design
* know about great artists, craft makers and designers, and understand the historical and cultural development of their art forms.

Attainment targets

By the end of each key stage, pupils are expected to know, apply and understand the matters, skills and processes specified in the relevant Programme of Study.

Schools are not required by law to teach the example content in the grey tint

Subject content

Key Stage 1

Pupils should be taught:

- to use a range of materials creatively to design and make products
- to use drawing, painting and sculpture to develop and share their ideas, experiences and imagination
- to develop a wide range of art and design techniques in using colour, pattern, texture, line, shape, form and space
- about the work of a range of artists, craft makers and designers, describing the differences and similarities between different practices and disciplines, and making links to their own work.

Key Stage 2

Pupils should be taught to develop their techniques, including their control and their use of materials, with creativity, experimentation and an increasing awareness of different kinds of art, craft and design.

Pupils should be taught:

- to create sketchbooks to record their observations and use them to review and revisit ideas
- to improve their mastery of art and design techniques, including drawing, painting and sculpture with a range of materials (eg pencil, charcoal, paint, clay)
- about great artists, architects and designers in history.

Computing

Purpose of study

A high-quality computing education equips pupils to use computational thinking and creativity to understand and change the world. Computing has deep links with mathematics, science and design and technology, and provides insights into both natural and artificial systems. The core of computing is computer science, in which pupils are taught the principals of information and computation, how digital systems work, and how to put this knowledge to use through programming. Building on this knowledge and understanding, pupils are equipped to use information technology to create programs, systems and a range of content. Computing also ensures that pupils become digitally literate - able to use, and express themselves and develop their ideas through, information and communication technology - at a level suitable for the future workplace and as active participants in a digital world.

Aims

The National Curriculum for computing aims to ensure that all pupils:

- can understand and apply the fundamental principles and concepts of computer science, including abstraction, logic, algorithms and data representation
- can analyse problems in computational terms, and have repeated practical experience of writing computer programs in order to solve such problems
- can evaluate and apply information technology, including new or unfamiliar technologies, analytically to solve problems
- are responsible, competent, confident and creative users of information and communication technology.

Attainment targets

By the end of each key stage, pupils are expected to know, apply and understand the matters, skills and processes specified in the relevant Programme of Study.

Schools are not required by law to teach the example content in the grey tint.

Subject content

Key Stage 1

Pupils should be taught to:

- understand what algorithms are; how they are implemented as programs on digital devices; and that programs execute by following precise and unambiguous instructions
- create and debug simple programs
- use logical reasoning to predict the behaviour of simple programs
- use technology purposefully to create, organise, store, manipulate and retrieve digital content
- recognise common uses of information technology beyond school.
- use technology safely and respectfully, keeping personal information private; identify where to go for help and support when they have concerns about content or contact on the Internet or other online technologies

Key Stage 2

Pupils should be taught to:

- design, write and debug programs that accomplish specific goals, including controlling or simulating physical systems; solve problems by decomposing them into smaller parts
- use sequence, selection and repetition in programs; work with variables and various forms of input and output
- use logical reasoning to explain how some simple algorithms work and to detect and correct errors in algorithms and programs
- understand computer networks including the Internet; how they can provide multiple services, such as the worldwide web; and the opportunities they offer for communication and collaboration
- use search technologies effectively, appreciate how results are selected and ranked, and be discerning in evaluating digital content
- select, use and combine a variety of software (including Internet services) on a range of digital devices to design and create a range of programs, systems and content that accomplish given goals, including collecting, analysing, evaluating and presenting data and information
- use technology safely, respectfully and responsibly; recognise acceptable/unacceptable behaviour; identify a range of ways to report concerns about content and contact

Design and technology

Purpose of study

Design and technology is an inspiring, rigorous and practical subject. Using creativity and imagination, pupils design and make products that solve real and relevant problems within a variety of contexts, considering their own and others' needs, wants and values. They acquire a broad range of subject knowledge and draw on disciplines such as mathematics, science, engineering, computing and art. Pupils learn how to take risks, becoming resourceful, innovative, enterprising and capable citizens. Through the evaluation of past and present design and technology, they develop a critical understanding of its impact on daily life and the wider world. High-quality design and technology education makes an essential contribution to the creativity, culture, wealth and well-being of the nation.

Aims

The National Curriculum for design and technology aims to ensure that all pupils:

- develop the creative, technical and practical expertise needed to perform everyday tasks confidently and to participate successfully in an increasingly technological world
- build and apply a repertoire of knowledge, understanding and skills in order to design and make high-quality prototypes and products for a wide range of users
- critique, evaluate and test their ideas and products and the work of others
- understand and apply the principles of nutrition and learn how to cook.

Attainment targets

By the end of each key stage, pupils are expected to know, apply and understand the matters, skills and processes specified in the relevant Programme of Study.

Schools are not required by law to teach the example content in the grey tint.

Subject content

Key Stage 1

Through a variety of creative and practical activities, pupils should be taught the knowledge, understanding and skills needed to engage in an iterative process of designing and making. They should work in a range of relevant contexts, for example, the home and school, gardens and playgrounds, the local community, industry and the wider environment.

When designing and making, pupils should be taught to:

Design

- design purposeful, functional, appealing products for themselves and other users based on design criteria
- generate, develop, model and communicate their ideas through talking, drawing, templates, mock-ups and, where appropriate, information and communication technology

Make

- select from and use a range of tools and equipment to perform practical tasks (for example, cutting, shaping, joining and finishing)
- select from and use a wide range of materials and components, including construction materials, textiles and ingredients, according to their characteristics

Evaluate

- explore and evaluate a range of existing products
- evaluate their ideas and products against design criteria

Technical knowledge

- build structures, exploring how they can be made stronger, stiffer and more stable
- explore and use mechanisms (for example, levers, sliders, wheels and axles), in their products.

Key Stage 2

Through a variety of creative and practical activities, pupils should be taught the knowledge, understanding and skills needed to engage in an iterative process of designing and making. They should work in a range of relevant contexts (for example, the home, school, leisure, culture, enterprise, industry and the wider environment).

When designing and making, pupils should be taught to:

Design

- use research and develop design criteria to inform the design of innovative, functional, appealing products that are fit for purpose, aimed at particular individuals or groups
- generate, develop, model and communicate their ideas through discussion, annotated sketches, cross-sectional and exploded diagrams, prototypes, pattern pieces and computer-aided design

Make

- select from and use a wider range of tools and equipment to perform practical tasks (for example, cutting, shaping, joining and finishing), accurately
- select from and use a wider range of materials and components, including construction materials, textiles and ingredients, according to their functional properties and aesthetic qualities

Evaluate

- investigate and analyse a range of existing products
- evaluate their ideas and products against their own design criteria and consider the views of others to improve their work
- understand how key events and individuals in design and technology have helped shape the world

Technical knowledge

- apply their understanding of how to strengthen, stiffen and reinforce more complex structures
- understand and use mechanical systems in their products (for example, gears, pulleys, cams, levers and linkages)
- understand and use electrical systems in their products (for example, series circuits incorporating switches, bulbs, buzzers and motors)
- apply their understanding of computing to programme, monitor and control their products.

Cooking and nutrition

As part of their work with food, pupils should be taught how to cook and apply the principles of nutrition and healthy eating. Instilling a love of cooking in pupils will also open a door to one of the great expressions of human creativity. Learning how to cook is a crucial life skill that enables pupils to feed themselves and others affordably and well, now and in later life.

Pupils should be taught to:

Key Stage 1

- use the basic principles of a healthy and varied diet to prepare dishes
- understand where food comes from.

Key Stage 2

- understand and apply the principles of a healthy and varied diet
- prepare and cook a variety of predominantly savoury dishes using a range of cooking techniques
- understand seasonality, and know where and how a variety of ingredients are grown, reared, caught and processed.

Geography

Purpose of study

A high-quality geography education should inspire in pupils a curiosity and fascination about the world and its people that will remain with them for the rest of their lives. Teaching should equip pupils with knowledge about diverse places, people, resources and natural and human environments, together with a deep understanding of the Earth's key physical and human processes. As pupils progress, their growing knowledge about the world should help them to deepen their understanding of the interaction between physical and human processes, and of the formation and use of landscapes and environments. Geographical knowledge, understanding and skills provide the frameworks and approaches that explain how the Earth's features at different scales are shaped, interconnected and change over time.

Aims

The National Curriculum for Geography aims to ensure that all pupils:

- develop contextual knowledge of the location of globally significant places - both terrestrial and marine - including their defining physical and human characteristics and how these provide geographical context for understanding the actions of processes
- understand the processes that give rise to key physical and human geographical features of the world, how these are interdependent and how they bring about spatial variation and change over time
- are competent in the geographical skills needed to:
  - collect, analyse and communicate with a range of data gathered through experiences of fieldwork that deepen their understanding of geographical processes
  - interpret a range of sources of geographical information, including maps, diagrams, globes, aerial photographs and Geographical Information Systems (GIS)
  - communicate geographical information in a variety of ways, including through maps and writing at length.

Attainment targets

By the end of each key stage, pupils are expected to know, apply and understand the matters, skills and processes specified in the relevant Programme of Study.

Schools are not required by law to teach the example content in the grey tint.

Subject content

Key Stage 1

Pupils should develop knowledge about the world, the United Kingdom and their locality. They should understand basic subject-specific vocabulary relating to human and physical geography and begin to use geographical skills, including first-hand observation, to enhance their locational awareness.

Pupils should be taught to:

Locational knowledge

- name and locate the world's seven continents and five oceans
- name, locate and identify characteristics of the four countries and capital cities of the United Kingdom and its surrounding seas

Place knowledge

- understand geographical similarities and differences through studying the human and physical geography of a small area of the United Kingdom, and of a small area in a contrasting non-European country

Human and physical geography

- identify seasonal and daily weather patterns in the United Kingdom and the location of hot and cold areas of the world in relation to the Equator and the North and South Poles
- use basic geographical vocabulary to refer to:
  - key physical features, including: beach, cliff, coast, forest, hill, mountain, sea, ocean, river, soil, valley, vegetation, season and weather
  - key human features, including: city, town, village, factory, farm, house, office, port, harbour and shop

Geographical skills and fieldwork

- use world maps, atlases and globes to identify the United Kingdom and its countries, as well as the countries, continents and oceans studied at this key stage
- use simple compass directions (North, South, East and West) and locational and directional language (for example, near and far; left and right) to describe the location of features and routes on a map
- use aerial photographs and plan perspectives to recognise landmarks and basic human and physical features; devise a simple map; and use and construct basic symbols in a key
- use simple fieldwork and observational skills to study the geography of their school and its grounds and the key human and physical features of its surrounding environment.

Key Stage 2

Pupils should extend their knowledge and understanding beyond the local area to include the United Kingdom and Europe, North and South America. This will include the location and characteristics of a range of the world's most significant human and physical features. They should develop their use of geographical tools and skills to enhance their locational and place knowledge.

Pupils should be taught to:

Locational knowledge

- locate the world's countries, using maps to focus on Europe (including the location of Russia) and North and South America, concentrating on their environmental regions, key physical and human characteristics, countries and major cities

- name and locate counties and cities of the United Kingdom, geographical regions and their identifying human and physical characteristics, key topographical features (including hills, mountains, coasts and rivers), and land-use patterns; and understand how some of these aspects have changed over time

- identify the position and significance of latitude, longitude, Equator, Northern Hemisphere, Southern Hemisphere, the Tropics of Cancer and Capricorn, Arctic and Antarctic Circle, the Prime/Greenwich Meridian and time zones (including day and night)

Place knowledge

- understand geographical similarities and differences through the study of human and physical geography of a region of the United Kingdom, a region in a European country, and a region within North or South America

Human and physical geography

- describe and understand key aspects of:
  - physical geography, including: climate zones, biomes and vegetation belts, rivers, mountains, volcanoes and earthquakes, and the water cycle
  - human geography, including: types of settlement and land use, economic activity including trade links, and the distribution of natural resources including energy, food, minerals and water

Geographical skills and fieldwork

- use maps, atlases, globes and digital/computer mapping to locate countries and describe features studied

- use the eight points of a compass, four and six-figure grid references, symbols and key (including the use of Ordnance Survey maps) to build their knowledge of the United Kingdom and the wider world

- use fieldwork to observe, measure and record the human and physical features in the local area using a range of methods, including sketch maps, plans and graphs and digital technologies.

History

Purpose of study

A high-quality history education will help pupils gain a coherent knowledge and understanding of Britain's past and that of the wider world. It should inspire pupils' curiosity to know more about the past. Teaching should equip pupils to ask perceptive questions, think critically, weigh evidence, sift arguments, and develop perspective and judgement. History helps pupils to understand the complexity of people's lives, the process of change, the diversity of societies and relationships between different groups, as well as their own identity and the challenges of their time.

Aims

The National Curriculum for history aims to ensure that all pupils:

- know and understand the history of these islands as a coherent, chronological narrative, from the earliest times to the present day: how people's lives have shaped this nation and how Britain has influenced and been influenced by the wider world
- know and understand significant aspects of the history of the wider world: the nature of ancient civilisations; the expansion and dissolution of empires; characteristic features of past non-European societies; achievements and follies of mankind
- gain and deploy a historically-grounded understanding of abstract terms such as *empire*, *civilisation*, *parliament* and *peasantry*
- understand historical concepts such as continuity and change, cause and consequence, similarity, difference and significance, and use them to make connections, draw contrasts, analyse trends, frame historically-valid questions and create their own structured accounts, including written narratives and analyses
- understand the methods of historical enquiry, including how evidence is used rigorously to make historical claims, and discern how and why contrasting arguments and interpretations of the past have been constructed
- gain historical perspective by placing their growing knowledge into different contexts, understanding the connections between local, regional, national and international history; between cultural, economic, military, political, religious and social history; and between short- and long-term timescales.

Attainment targets

By the end of each key stage, pupils are expected to know, apply and understand the matters, skills and processes specified in the relevant Programme of Study.

Schools are not required by law to teach the example content in the grey tint.

Subject content

Key Stage 1

Pupils should develop an awareness of the past, using common words and phrases relating to the passing of time. They should know where the people and events they study fit within a chronological framework and identify similarities and differences between ways of life in different periods. They should use a wide vocabulary of everyday historical terms. They should ask and answer questions, choosing and using parts of stories and other sources to show that they know and understand key features of events. They should understand some of the ways in which we find out about the past and identify different ways in which it is represented.

In planning to ensure the progression described above through teaching about the people, events and changes outlined below, teachers are often introducing pupils to historical periods that they will study more fully at Key Stages 2 and 3.

Pupils should be taught about:

- changes within living memory. Where appropriate, these should be used to reveal aspects of change in national life
- events beyond living memory that are significant nationally or globally (for example, the Great Fire of London, the first aeroplane flight or events commemorated through festivals or anniversaries)
- the lives of significant individuals in the past who have contributed to national and international achievements. Some should be used to compare aspects of life in different periods (for example, Elizabeth I and Queen Victoria, Christopher Columbus and Neil Armstrong, William Caxton and Tim Berners-Lee, Pieter Bruegel the Elder and LS Lowry, Rosa Parks and Emily Davison, Mary Seacole and/or Florence Nightingale and Edith Cavell)
- significant historical events, people and places in their own locality.

Key Stage 2

Pupils should continue to develop a chronologically secure knowledge and understanding of British, local and world history, establishing clear narratives within and across the periods they study. They should note connections, contrasts and trends over time and develop the appropriate use of historical terms. They should regularly address and sometimes devise historically valid questions about change, cause, similarity and difference, and significance. They should construct informed responses that involve thoughtful selection and organisation of relevant historical information. They should understand how our knowledge of the past is constructed from a range of sources.

In planning to ensure the progression described above through teaching the British, local and world history outlined below, teachers should combine overview and depth studies to help pupils understand both the long arc of development and the complexity of specific aspects of the content.

Pupils should be taught about:

- changes in Britain from the Stone Age to the Iron Age

  This could include:

  - late Neolithic hunter-gatherers and early farmers, for example, Skara Brae
  - Bronze Age religion, technology and travel, for example, Stonehenge
  - Iron Age hill forts: tribal kingdoms, farming, art and culture

- the Roman Empire and its impact on Britain

  This could include:

  - Julius Caesar's attempted invasion in 55–54BC
  - the Roman Empire by AD42 and the power of its army
  - successful invasion by Claudius and conquest, including Hadrian's Wall
  - British resistance, for example, Boudica
  - 'Romanisation' of Britain: sites such as Caerwent and the impact of technology, culture and beliefs, including early Christianity

- Britain's settlement by Anglo-Saxons and Scots

  This could include:

  - Roman withdrawal from Britain in c AD410 and the fall of the western Roman Empire
  - Scots' invasions from Ireland to north Britain (now Scotland)
  - Anglo-Saxon invasions, settlements and kingdoms: place names and village life
  - Anglo-Saxon art and culture
  - Christian conversion – Canterbury, Iona and Lindisfarne

- the Viking and Anglo-Saxon struggle for the Kingdom of England to the time of Edward the Confessor

  This could include:

  - Viking raids and invasion
  - resistance by Alfred the Great and Athelstan, first king of England
  - further Viking invasions and Danegeld
  - Anglo-Saxon laws and justice
  - Edward the Confessor and his death in 1066

- a local history study

  For example:

  - a depth study linked to one of the British areas of study listed above
  - a study over time tracing how several aspects of national history are reflected in the locality (this can go beyond 1066)
  - a study of an aspect of history or a site dating from a period beyond 1066 that is significant in the locality

- a study of an aspect or theme in British history that extends pupils' chronological knowledge beyond 1066

  For example:
  - the changing power of monarchs, using case studies such as John, Anne and Victoria
  - changes in an aspect of social history, such as crime and punishment from the Anglo-Saxons to the present or leisure and entertainment in the 20th century
  - the legacy of Greek or Roman culture (art, architecture or literature) on later periods in British history, including the present day
  - a significant turning point in British history (for example, the first railways or the Battle of Britain)

- the achievements of the earliest civilizations – an overview of where and when the first civilizations appeared and a depth study of one of the following: Ancient Sumer; the Indus Valley; Ancient Egypt; the Shang Dynasty of Ancient China

- Ancient Greece – a study of Greek life and achievements and their influence on the western world

- a non-European society that provides contrasts with British history – one study chosen from: early Islamic civilization, including a study of Baghdad *c* AD900; Mayan civilization *c* AD900; Benin (West Africa) *c* AD900–1300.

Languages

Purpose of study

Learning a foreign language is a liberation from insularity and provides an opening to other cultures. A high-quality languages education should foster pupils' curiosity and deepen their understanding of the world. The teaching should enable pupils to express their ideas and thoughts in another language and to understand and respond to its speakers, both in speech and in writing. It should also provide opportunities for them to communicate for practical purposes, learn new ways of thinking and read great literature in the original language. Language teaching should provide the foundation for learning further languages, equipping pupils to study and work in other countries.

Aims

The National Curriculum for languages aims to ensure that all pupils:

- understand and respond to spoken and written language from a variety of authentic sources
- speak with increasing confidence, fluency and spontaneity, finding ways of communicating what they want to say, including through discussion and asking questions, and continually improving the accuracy of their pronunciation and intonation
- can write at varying length, for different purposes and audiences, using the variety of grammatical structures that they have learned
- discover and develop an appreciation of a range of writing in the language studied.

Attainment targets

By the end of each key stage, pupils are expected to know, apply and understand the matters, skills and processes specified in the relevant Programme of Study.

Schools are not required by law to teach the example content in the grey tint.

Subject content

Key Stage 2: Foreign languages

Teaching may be of any modern or ancient foreign language and should focus on enabling pupils to make substantial progress in one language. The teaching should provide an appropriate balance of spoken and written language and should lay the foundations for further foreign language teaching at Key Stage 3. It should enable pupils to understand and communicate ideas, facts and feelings in speech and writing, focused on familiar and routine matters, using their knowledge of phonology, grammatical structures and vocabulary.

The focus of study in modern languages will be on practical communication. If an ancient language is chosen, the focus will be to provide a linguistic foundation for reading comprehension and an appreciation of classical civilisation. Pupils studying ancient languages may take part in simple oral exchanges, while discussion of what they read will be conducted in English. A linguistic foundation in ancient languages may support the study of modern languages at key stage 3.

Pupils should be taught to:

- listen attentively to spoken language and show understanding by joining in and responding
- explore the patterns and sounds of language through songs and rhymes, and link the spelling, sound and meaning of words
- engage in conversations; ask and answer questions; express opinions and respond to those of others; seek clarification and help*
- speak in sentences, using familiar vocabulary, phrases and basic language structures
- develop accurate pronunciation and intonation so that others understand when they are reading aloud or using familiar words and phrases*
- present ideas and information orally to a range of audiences*
- read carefully and show understanding of words, phrases and simple writing
- appreciate stories, songs, poems and rhymes in the language
- broaden their vocabulary and develop their ability to understand new words that are introduced into familiar written material, including through using a dictionary
- write phrases from memory, and adapt these to create new sentences, to express ideas clearly
- describe people, places, things and actions orally* and in writing
- understand basic grammar appropriate to the language being studied, including (where relevant): feminine, masculine and neuter forms and the conjugation of high-frequency verbs; key features and patterns of the language; how to apply these, for instance, to build sentences; and how these differ from or are similar to English.

The starred (*) content above will not be applicable to ancient languages.

Music

Purpose of study

Music is a universal language that embodies one of the highest forms of creativity. A high-quality music education should engage and inspire pupils to develop a love of music and their talent as musicians, and so increase their self-confidence, creativity and sense of achievement. As pupils progress, they should develop a critical engagement with music, allowing them to compose, and to listen with discrimination to the best in the musical canon.

Aims

The National Curriculum for music aims to ensure that all pupils:

- perform, listen to, review and evaluate music across a range of historical periods, genres, styles and traditions, including the works of the great composers and musicians

- learn to sing and to use their voices, to create and compose music on their own and with others, have the opportunity to learn a musical instrument, use technology appropriately and have the opportunity to progress to the next level of musical excellence

- understand and explore how music is created, produced and communicated, including through the interrelated dimensions: pitch, duration, dynamics, tempo, timbre, texture, structure and appropriate musical notations.

Attainment targets

By the end of each key stage, pupils are expected to know, apply and understand the matters, skills and processes specified in the relevant Programme of Study.

Subject content

Key Stage 1

Pupils should be taught to:

- use their voices expressively and creatively by singing songs and speaking chants and rhymes
- play tuned and untuned instruments musically
- listen with concentration and understanding to a range of high-quality live and recorded music
- experiment with, create, select and combine sounds using the interrelated dimensions of music.

Key Stage 2

Pupils should be taught to sing and play musically with increasing confidence and control. They should develop an understanding of musical composition, organising and manipulating ideas within musical structures and reproducing sounds from aural memory.

Pupils should be taught to:

- play and perform in solo and ensemble contexts, using their voices and playing musical instruments with increasing accuracy, fluency, control and expression
- improvise and compose music for a range of purposes using the interrelated dimensions of music
- listen with attention to detail and recall sounds with increasing aural memory
- use and understand staff and other musical notations
- appreciate and understand a wide range of high-quality live and recorded music drawn from different traditions and from great composers and musicians
- develop an understanding of the history of music.

Physical Education

Purpose of study

A high-quality physical education curriculum inspires all pupils to succeed and excel in competitive sport and other physically demanding activities. It should provide opportunities for pupils to become physically confident in a way which supports their health and fitness. Opportunities to compete in sport and other activities build character and help to embed values such as fairness and respect.

Aims

The National Curriculum for physical education aims to ensure that all pupils:

- develop competence to excel in a broad range of physical activities
- are physically active for sustained periods of time
- engage in competitive sports and activities
- lead healthy, active lives.

Attainment targets

By the end of each key stage, pupils are expected to know, apply and understand the matters, skills and processes specified in the relevant Programme of Study.

Schools are not required by law to teach the example content in the grey tint.

Subject content

Key Stage 1

Pupils should develop fundamental movement skills, become increasingly competent and confident, and access a broad range of opportunities to extend their agility, balance and coordination, individually and with others. They should be able to engage in competitive (both against self and against others) and cooperative physical activities, in a range of increasingly challenging situations.

Pupils should be taught to:

- master basic movements including running, jumping, throwing and catching, as well as developing balance, agility and coordination, and begin to apply these in a range of activities
- participate in team games, developing simple tactics for attacking and defending
- perform dances using simple movement patterns.

Key Stage 2

Pupils should continue to apply and develop a broader range of skills, learning how to use them in different ways and to link them to make actions and sequences of movement. They should enjoy communicating, collaborating and competing with each other. They should develop an understanding of how to improve in different physical activities and sports and learn how to evaluate and recognise their own success.

Pupils should be taught to:

- use running, jumping, throwing and catching in isolation and in combination
- play competitive games, modified where appropriate (for example, adminton, basketball, cricket, football, hockey, netball, rounders and tennis), and apply basic principles suitable for attacking and defending
- develop flexibility, strength, technique, control and balance (for example through athletics and gymnastics)
- perform dances using a range of movement patterns
- take part in outdoor and adventurous activity challenges both individually and within a team
- compare their performances with previous ones and demonstrate improvement to achieve their personal best.

Swimming and water safety

All schools must provide swimming instruction either in key stage 1 or Key Stage 2. In particular, pupils should be taught to:

- swim competently, confidently and proficiently over a distance of at least 25 metres
- use a range of strokes effectively (for example, front crawl, backstroke and breaststroke)
- perform safe self-rescue in different water-based situations.

Notes

Notes

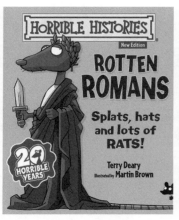

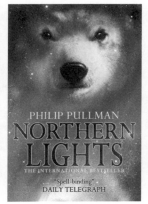
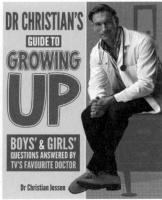
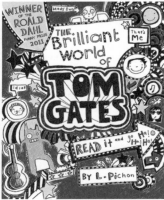